CONTENTS

INTRODUCTION

I've always felt a special bond with Mata Hari and Garrison Keillor. And with Billie Burke, who played Glinda the Good Witch in *The Wizard of Oz*. And also with B.J. Thomas, who sang the immortal song "Raindrops Keep Fallin' on My Head."

Why? Not because I have an urge to become a spy or a folksy storyteller, or because I go around saying "Just click your heels three times ..."—and certainly not because I have any musical ability.

No, the thing that ties me to the above celebrities (and, incidentally, to such others as John Glover, Stan Freberg, and Ralph Bunche) is completely accidental: We were all born on August 7. Different years, of course.

With whom do you share a birthday? Whatever day of the year it is, this book provides you with a quotation from one of your personal "birthday-mates." The cryptogram for January 1 was said by a celebrity born on January 1. The May 15 quotation was from someone born on May 15. On December 31 is a quote from someone born on ... well, you get the idea. For those few of you actually born on February 29, we even have a February 29 bonus celebrity quotation for you.

So, check out your birthday quote. Then decide whether to ration yourself to one cryptogram per day, or whether to gobble up all the celebrity musings in less time. Either way, a full year's worth of ponderings from the rich and famous await.

—Trip Payne

HOW TO USE THIS BOOK

Cryptograms are sentences in code. Each letter of the alphabet has been replaced by another letter. A letter is replaced by the same "replacement letter" throughout the code. For example:

```
G  R  Y  P  Y     H  P  A  M  P  A  G  P  H

C  O  D  E  D     S  E  N  T  E  N  C  E  S
```

Here, each of the two G's stands for C, while R stands for O, and so on. The code patterns change with each puzzle; if X stands for A in one cryptogram, it may stand for a different letter in the next cryptogram. A letter can never stand for itself.

There are a number of little clues that can help you crack a cryptogram. For example:

A one-letter word is always going to be A or I.

A word with an apostrophe before the last letter is going to end in N'T (like CAN'T), 'M (I'M), 'S (MAN'S), or 'D (HE'D). Two letters after an apostrophe might be 'LL (WE'LL), 'VE (I'VE), or 'RE (THEY'RE).

Certain common words have distinct letter patterns. For example: DID, THAT, NEVER, LITTLE, and PEOPLE.

Also, certain words are going to come up over and over simply because they're so commonly written and spoken. Keep a watchful eye out for THE, AND, NOT, YOU, and WITH, for example. In addition, look out for words ending in -ED, -ING, -LESS, -NESS, and -TION.

If you need help, there are two sets of hints in the back. The first set will tell you the profession of the person who said the quotation, as well as the year the celebrity was born. The second set of hints will give you a more direct hint about a letter or word in the puzzle.

Each set of hints is arranged so that you won't accidentally see a hint for the next cryptogram. All of the "1st"s are first: January 1, February 1, March 1, and so on. Then January 2, February 2, etc.

If you're still puzzled, you can check out the index, which gives the name of every celebrity who's quoted in the book! (Don't look now. You're not stumped yet, are you?)

And then, of course, you can always peek at the answers, which are in normal order. I won't tell.

January 1

NGEEAER MHN ILB ONBCAXBEPS AC CHTBILAER
VADB INSAER IH CIUEX GO AE U LUTTHPD.

—JUNNS RHVXFUIBN

January 2

GRUP RI ZGPLILAN. JPLNY RI ZPLKPUHG. RN'I
NYP NBLAIRNRCA NYLN'I NBCHOGPICWP.

—RILLK LIRWCQ

January 3

AF BO ORHDL A PNFDTE DR IT N SUTND
GNFDRBABAWD, IHD A MRHFE A LNE FRDLAFS DR
WNO.   —JAKDRU IRUST

January 4

MY M KLRO VOOF LVCO BN GOO YLABKOA BKLF
NBKOAG, MB TLG VOXLZGO M GBNNP NF BKO
GKNZCPOAG NY JMLFBG.   —MGLLX FOTBNF

8

January 5

MO TVL BHD ILHD TVL LPUDHISBPU
DRDHTSWMPX SWBS MI XVMPX VP, TVL BHD
WVZDNDIINT QVPOLIDU.   —JBNSDH YVPUBND

January 6

DBIHN TD BIHNLINX FRTJR GIVXD AEE TGD
JAIG, DWTGD AH TGD RIHKD, IHK NAXD GA
FAOV.   —JIOB DIHKQLON

January 7

CD TMM MGOW XGY MGKD. CRDURDY CD JOGC BU
GY OGU, DKDYZURBOW DMAD CD QG BA FIAU
JBMMBOW UBVD.   —JDOOZ MGWWBOA

January 8

YIYO PO COY'L CHO TFYT CN YJKYFMPLY, MRY
DCOZYF XCE LMEUX TOU LKYAPTDPBY, MRY QCFY
XCE SOCH TWCEM DYLL TOU DYLL.

—ARTFDYL CLZCCU

9

January 9

CT YF CFECKCERYH PYFSO SG ZL Y HLYELI YFE
COF'S VGFSIGKLIOCYH, SWYS JLYFO WL FLKLI
OSGGE TGI YFBSWCFN. —ICVWYIE J. FCMGF

···

January 10

P FLIG GR JZZN WPYAGPIY UZXLDKZ PG PK GAZ
RIES GAPIY GALG JZZNK QZ RDG RW GAZ
ALQUDCYZC VRPIGK. —YZRCYZ WRCZQLI

···

January 11

HULPL DF BGAX BGL HUDGK C TUDABFBTULP
QCG WL PLADLN BG HB NB, CGN HUCH DF HB
QBGHPCNDQH BHULP TUDABFBTULPF.

—JDAADCR VCRLF

···

January 12

VT BYJ'DN SYVES MY PY FYRNMCVES MYEVSCM
BYJ'GG WN FYDDB TYD MYRYDDYK RYDEVES,
FGNNQ GXMN. —CNEEB BYJESRXE

January 13

JX TIX LHG FHOBULK GEX XZHLHQW TLR JX TIX

LHG ZCIULK ZTLZXI. JX TIX SCFG GIWULK GH

QTAX T KHHR SHAX.   —SCOUT OHCUF-RIXWNCF

January 14

DA'VA FOO LVJHB JZ KFRPUY OPSSOA

KPWSFRAW. PS YPGAW HW SXA ZAAOPUY DA

BJU'S KFRA FUT QPY JUAW.   —FUBT VJJUAT

January 15

RT JGHFU BRBU'Z FLREZ, NPP ZWF HGUFX RU

ZWF JGCPB JGMPB WNKF UG HFNURUS.

—NCREZGZPF GUNEERE

January 16

VMTVGK HJBO FWOY FWO CMZ NJPO, OBOR TWOR

GCL NOOM MJDO V KALVKWOZ QVDO CN JQO.

—OFWOM YOPYVR

....
January 17

MS TNG CNGVE VMFB AN FRNC AUB OQVGB NS
YNRBT, ZN QRE AHT AN XNHHNC INYB.

— XBRWQYMR SHQRFVMR

....
January 18

A BURKRPORO KN MR CNHRMNOW A LSPKRO KN
MR JPKAT A GAPSTTW MRVSHR KISK BRUCNP—
NU IR MRVSHR HR.   — VSUW QUSPK

....
January 19

HN FRAX CS GEX KBBA XECO SGES SGBZ TGH
YHXS OCXMCVB SGBY EWB MBEXS EKMB SH
RSSBW SGBY.   — BOLEW EMMEA FHB

....
January 20

T BLYMEK LGJO ZOOF G PYMFNSV-COBNOSF
BTFROS. GQNOS GEE, T'D YEKOS NLGF DYBN
COBNOSF PYMFNSTOB.   — ROYSRO ZMSFB

January 21

FDU VQOUW TVX KUF, FDU MFWVCKUW FDU JHCO

KUFM—RCO HF'M RQJRTM HC TVXW PRIU.

—BRIN CHINQRXM

January 22

TWY TQ DOY KGYPRIBYR TQ BYPAVWC TGA

GYDDYBR VR DOY JWTFGYACY DOPD DOYN WYYA

WT PWRFYB.   —CYTBCY CTBATW MNBTW

January 23

DAHPH LPH YHZHP DHY MLGO DT FT

OTJHDARYK, TYBG TYH. DALD RO L XCHODRTY

TV JTPLBRDG.   —SHLYYH JTPHLC

January 24

MP EAKS HT'U QNED NOSMAZ NE JT CBDDS,

HT'U CBGT B DOTNNS ZEEU NMVT.

—TUMNC HCBONEA

January 25

WISES YES WIESS EPKSO QTE NEXWXJR Y JTZSK.

PJQTEWPJYWSKM, JT TJS GJTNO NIYW WISM

YES.   —N. OTVSEOSW VYPRIYV

January 26

L HZUO'S FILMBO SE ZJSLOK QC ZO LOOBI

JEVXYWULEO. L HZU IYOOLOK ZHZC PIEV SGB

UXEISLOK KEEFU QYULOBUU.   —XZYW OBHVZO

January 27

GS TVL CGOGE TVLW HUEGVFA GF CGSZ EV

EPGFKA EPHE FVXVQT UHF BVAAGXCT SGFQ

SHLCE JGEP, TVL JGCC FVE QV OLUP.

                              —CZJGA UHWWVCC

January 28

B AM TMY YPE YM AVTLG JGYYGP YKVT VTEMTG

GHUG. B MTHE YPE YM AVTLG JGYYGP YKVT

DEUGHC.   —DBIKVBH JVPEUKTBIMX

January 29

CEXPD JVP GHZP PGPIFJDSM SE XP; SFPQ'VP
DHRP SE GEEZ JS YKS H CEKGBD'S CJDS SE ECD
EDP.   —C.R. AHPGBM

January 30

B GNBFY DC LPFQBMCJ GPP HTLN GNC RPPM
VTLY PK GNC CXJVS ZBJM XFM FPG CFPTRN GNC
ZXM VTLY PK GNC CXJVS DPJH.

                          —KJXFYVBF M. JPPQCWCVG

January 31

KE'D EPM CBBW CKXGD TPB FMMY EPM
WKUXKMD; EPM JUW CKXGD QMZMX PUZM EPM
EKNM.   —EUGGLGUP JUQFPMUW

February 1

FWY SKUP BYCGSK FWYP VSJY FS GYY JY TG
FWCF T HKSX FWCF UTMY TG NBYCF—CKQ FWYP
HKSX T HKSX TF.   —VUCBH NCAUY

GLU LPSHUAG GLFBZ GC UDQEPFB FA GLU

ZEPSFBZEK UJFHUBG RLFML UJUSKNCHK LPH

HUMFHUH BCG GC AUU.   —PKB SPBH

WAWFZQELZ PWGK KE BNVD TXREFBUGTEX UOO

LUZ OEXP GDUG GDWZ OEKW GDWTF VEBBEX

KWXKW.   —PWFGFNLW KGWTX

PNE HNK BZOS OI OGRNVSWXS—BIRBYOWDDH OT

HNK'VB SPOXLOXA NT YNGOXA UWYL.

                          —JWX FKWHDB

OH DMBFYK BN YHD TRY NDJOKOFDN FRD TRDOF

LKYX FRD WROLL OHM JKBHFN FRD WROLL.

                          —OMGOB NFDZDHNYH

February 6

FBQHR POQ'S TER XODDZQHLL TES ZS CZAA
PHJSOZQAR WHS RBE O THSSHJ PAOLL BK
FHFBJZHL. —JBQOAV JHOWOQ

February 7

WJAN FEWITFR EF TWY UEEAY; WJAN
NCNDZWITFR EF NCTQNFPN. WINDN'Y FE
LNWWND DHUN. —PIJDUNY QTPANFY

February 8

MT QCN EGMZV ME'I GUBY EC PLLE ZLD JLCJFL,
EBQ JMHVMZW NJ EGL DBCZW WCFT XUFF.

—RUHV FLPPCZ

February 9

WOSR OL QRNNRA NTGF ERGNT, O QRWORJR, OS
DFWZ QRMGXLR ON OL WRLL QDAOFH GFE
QRMGXLR ON TGL SARLT BRGMTRL OF ON.

—GWOMR CGWPRA

February 10

LGH APLWEVLH NC QHWXS MAZZHMMCAP WM LGH

PAKAUT NC SWFWXS TNAUMHPC LGH LWEH LN JN

BGVL TNA BVXL LN JN.   —PHNXLTXH DUWZH

··

February 11

QN QWZARF HOR YXR MATE YXRN FXWP AT

COAFWTF HTE WT HAOCGHTRF JRKHDFR TWJWEN

KHT GRHZR.   —JDOY ORNTWGEF

··

February 12

SAYZ KTH ANRY JTC NZ YVYQANZC DK CAY AOZI

VYJW NZI AY OW CEKOZJ CT EHZ NSNK, OC OW

DYWC CT VYC AOP EHZ.   —NDENANP VOZXTVZ

··

February 13

MCA BWWY MCHUB PEWGM MCA KWXHAL HL MCPM

QWG OPU APM PUY KAYHMPMA PM MCA LPKA

MHKA.   —BAWIBA LABPV

February 14

FNIX OX OC FHRP JRSLK, PVXKM TNV, TEY T

LXTSBNPSR ATVBEXV, TEY CHS JTE QXXA OC

FHRP JRSLK TEY BMX PVXKM TNV. —ZTJQ LXEEC

February 15

XPB XY GV WOHBY ABRABSK EFAHPR GV VBLAK

HP SOB SOBLSBA HK SOLS H WXFJEP'S KHS HP

SOB LFEHBPWB LPE MLSWO GB.

—QXOP CLAAVGXAB

February 16

RBLQ TDLM VAZAL MHPPAQ BVOWDQO, WYE TRO

EBMA B GRBVGA DV WAHVS ERA CHLNE?

—AQSBL WALSAV

February 17

Z'D ORN RHN NILKL YMLPNZOQ TRK NIKLL

IRHKY LWLKE GPE FHYN NR TZOG RHN MIPN ZN

TLLXY XZVL NR YMLPN. —DZJIPLX FRKGPO

February 18

PN SGAJA PD W ZFFB TFV JAWMMT HWKS SF
JAWL ZVS PS GWDK'S ZAAK HJPSSAK TAS, SGAK
TFV CVDS HJPSA PS. —SFKP CFJJPDFK

February 19

BGRM TD CMSMUOBBJ ROBXME OA TAD NTCNMDA
EXUTSC AHG KMUTGED TS BTWM: ANM EOJD GW
FGXUATSC OSE ANM EOJD TS FGXUA.

—BMM LOURTS

February 20

REJEKA TLD BQBG NLKB L FEEK NEQOB.
DENBKLA DENBERB HOSS NLVB TLSP L FEEK
ERB. —GEJBGC LSCNLR

February 21

JOPH AC FLYZ GPUMAP JLXY WHY THVTXC, L TZP
W HLUP, ZWBP QXWCQPH. JOPH DOPC'VP
BLHLZOPY, L UXLAG MTD. —PVAW GMAGPUF

February 22

R SFESHJ WSK VY VYGOW VWM JVYAM VY JMM

WYE WYV RV ESJ. R ESJ ZMAMX YZM YD VWYJM

EWY OYGFK LGJV WMSX SNYGV RV.

—KXME NSXXHTYXM

February 23

TDMPOWL DE TPC JUPD YLKQWUD JL ZPMMQLY

GLEGKL UPAL DE TLL DULTL GEEM BEEKT

YLRECLY QODE EHM REOYQDQEO.

—TPZHLK GLGCT

February 24

RYDOHRD GYG DHE VZQM Z TMK FYEM ZE

EVM RHS OZKYD TVMAM VYF JZAMDEF

VHUM-FOVHHRMG VYU, ZDG VM EBADMG HBE

JAMEEX YDEMAMFEYDS.   —FEMQM CHKF

February 25

JFNOK FVE AKL BHUJE JFNOKT BYAK MHN;

TVHUL FVE MHN TJLLD FJHVL.

—FVAKHVM CNUOLTT

21

··

February 26

FIFCO VARF A JAEK N ZACW TYD PNE PDDU

WAUF RO RDVYFC, MYF WDDUM WAUF RO

JNVYFC.   —VDEO CNEKNWW

··

February 27

WAO HUNCOTTBNY NC KNNV PUBWBYE FIVOT

ANUTO UILBYE TOOF QBVO I TNQBJ, TWIKQO

KXTBYOTT.   —SNAY TWOBYKOLV

··

February 28

HEYLM UNYMER OF LWCLRF CEOMMYD AR

FNJYANGR FMELODODH MN HN AYRNDG CSLM SY

TLD GN.   —FMYUSYD FUYDGYE

··

February 29

TLR SHLLTA FCYER "VTJRLEPWL" ZPTU H ZWPBA

JRHPWLE, HLY W SRPAHWLVQ YT LTA WLARLY AT

JRHP WA H BRSTLY AWUR.

                                 —EWTHSSJWLT PTBBWLW

March 1

BWIVI'L JFBWUJM GVFJM GUBW BIIJPMIVL BWPB

VIPLFJUJM GUBW BWIY GFJ'B PMMVDPBI.

—VFJ WFGPVS

March 2

VF LKBUP VF'YF BU LKF ZYFJFUL, HNL VF

WYFU'L. LKF ZYFJFUL VF PUGV BJ GUDA W

RGXBF GQ LKF ZWJL.   —LGR VGDQF

March 3

VIL TBGLY FHRL GL SLAMOPL H CBY'V FBBR

FHRL M KHXF TIB TBOFC PVLMF M IOPSMYC—MV

FLMPV YBV QBX FBYK.   —DLMY IMXFBT

March 4

TUM BTDD WD FTTK JTH ARM DTPB. ATT ZCUS

BTDDMD CHM UTA FTTK JTH ARM YTCYR.

—VUPAM HTYVUM

23

March 5

KRBSODOG JS JF SRBS XBTOF B COGFLY

WRBGXJYZ, JS YOOUF SL GOXBJY B XPFSOGP.

—GOM RBGGJFLY

March 6

S WLCP GERTE TWLN SN TLY KSGP NR OP

WHEIAD, OHN S LKTLDY TPEN ASIWN NR L

APYNLHALEN.   —ASEI KLAFEPA

March 7

B'D CBCLX-CBOW, B'D HOWUJWBIQL, B'D

VTPYQWTYWY, B'D AHUGX—TGY B'D HG LHE HC

LQW QWTE.   —JBPPTUY FAHLL

March 8

I JBING LONU OJ EHD MTE FHEMJ TEM GE QUIW

GDHHOJ, QOIHE, IHY YRBP.   —UWHH NDYLNICD

March 9

D TXBSUX BR RPFUPHU TNP DOTDIR RUOOR. DH
DJSNPX BR PHU TNP TXBSUR D CPPM SNDS
FDMUR D CBE RKODRN.   —FBQMUI RKBOODHU

March 10

BASBTA GUZA FPULPAK PS WUTT DA DQFF
FPSHA QHFPAUK SJ VMFP FGULSH, CGQWG Q'D
FMLA QF U WSDYQHUPQSH SJ DN UEA UHK DN
UPPQPMKA.   —FGULSH FPSHA

March 11

MUP GBOLDDGWEP LIMPT UYD Y RGTH LI
GTMPNAGMX CUGVU MUP BPAPEX GBOALWYWEP
EYVRD.   —HLZNEYD YHYBD

March 12

X'A GZDXUM GB OY F CLOPXI NXMLZY FUE FG
GKY JFAY GXAY OY FWYZFMY. XG'J PXVY
CZBIPFXAXUM AD BZEXUFZXUYJJ.

—QFAYJ GFDPBZ

25

March 13

RPZZLTAYY LY GRA MJABQMILTD MX TMG

KTSTMOT MVYGPQHAY GMOPBW P STMOT DMPH.

—H. BMT RKVVPBW

March 14

EWKS GQE GUFWAX CHY FWJFWFGY, GUY

PWFRYHXY CWZ UPDCW XGPOFZFGS, CWZ F'D

WEG XPHY CMEPG GUY JEHDYH.

—CKMYHG YFWXGYFW

March 15

GU G BLBY OBBMBM V NYVGO FYVOCWTVOF, G'M

IRKKCB V CWKYFCXYGFBY NBIVHCB G'M XVOF V

NYVGO FRVF RVM OBLBY NBBO HCBM.

—OKYA LVO NYKIPTGO

March 16

CRACFR PLOR JR GRELTDR W LJ L

JTFOWZLERORB, OLFRQORB, HRLFOPS,

WQORUQLOWAQLFFS ZLJATD XRQWTD.

—KRUUS FRHWD

March 17

P'OW LPOWR BD BWBSPQG THQ BSQW NESVLEN
NEHR HRD ST BD BHQQPHLWG. DSV KHR'N
XPOSQKW H FSSM.   —LYSQPH GCHRGSR

March 18

S CWSPOCD USPW SYBPO GTFW JTRNBUWN WSJC
DWSF TRW SRY S CSPK OHUWN CHN TLR LWHVCO
HR TOCWFN' ISOHWRJW.   —ZTCR BIYHQW

March 19

OS TDCHOLT CGCHUPEOSJ JBCK TSR SBPEOSJ
DTPPCHK, ZEOVC OS CXHBFC SBPEOSJ JBCK TSR
CGCHUPEOSJ DTPPCHK.   —FEOVOF HBPE

March 20

THL GKHLAV BOXOM SODM THLM ROGE
EMHLGOMG SKOB THL WH HLE EH NPWKE NHM
APROMET DBV EMLEK.   —KOBMPC PRGOB

March 21

Q'F UNX XAM OQUS NZ HMYCNU JAN'S BMX V

WNNO VUS V XYVQUMY. QZ Q SN, WVGG FM KH

VUS YMFQUS FM JAVX Q LKCX CVQS.

—YNCQM N'SNUUMGG

March 22

W JECNCE GCMEQAWY JCQJDC. W DWVC AQ KCBE

EMLIDWGOH ICGCBAK AKC HMENBYC.

—HACJKCG HQGFKCWL

March 23

SKYA QX C LQMA, PHZ JOAZOAM QZ QX DKQED

ZK JCMF TKHM OACMZO KM PHME VKJE TKHM

OKHXA, TKH WCE EAYAM ZASS.

—GKCE WMCJLKMV

March 24

L'M STAKUS RTXU VC LF AKU GLMMEU BZ

FBRKUSU AKTF LF TFD NLAD BF UTSAK.

—PAUJU GNIVUUF

March 25

JDUBU'C YVGL V WUCJCUMMUB JDVJ OKXMH

DVQU WUUG ZBUQUGJUH WL V FKKH JUVODUB.

                              —PMVGGUBL K'OKGGKB

March 26

AF UNGDOQT CHOYMCESSF ROTMY MNEGL H WHF,

FNE PHF RZRQYEHSSF TRY YN AR ANLL HQW

UNGD YURSZR MNEGL H WHF.   —GNARGY CGNLY

March 27

C ESPHM JGFD PKPGNSVCWX. XGPHS HGSCESE

ESPHM; SVPN QFW'S QF VFDHXPE.

                              —BRPWSCW SHGHWSCWF

March 28

LOPZ V QR KZ XW-SPJWR TRZM, V OKYP SR JKIP

VS NVNS NVIP K LRJKZ LVNN SLVTS LOPZ TOP'T

LKNIVZM QRLZ SOP TSUPPS.   —UPGK JHPZSVUP

29

March 29

MONY QHS-QHUW NHIWSN, TFD YHCW NF MFKE

CWKT YHKU. MONY BFU-BOCWS NHIWSN, TFD

GDXN NFDJY ON DR FSJW OS H MYOIW.

—RWHKI PHOIWT

March 30

O'D BAY. O'D EBFSH. O'D OSLMAAOHMSL. O'D

XLFJOY. DE LOYM HBMX OS TSY BFL.

—VTPPMS KMTLLE

March 31

RIMB KCA IWTM LIM PWNLD CB KCAO DGZM,

WOJAM LIM PWNLD. RIMB KCA IWTM LIM FWR CB

KCAO DGZM, WOJAM LIM FWR. RIMB KCA IWTM

BMGLIMO, ICFFMO.   —WF JCOM

April 1

GX KCYVO FHEOOE CHD WOOM ROLYZOR ZY

BOOTUMA TOYTVO JEYG BMYKUMA GO.

—VYM FCHMOX

April 2

Y OD PAYLPS SGOLX JFK, TWP Y LGOK OP PAG

PAYLPS-CJWL-SGOL-JFK FGNGF. —KOZO HOLNGS

April 3

KYG BGCUUS JBLNYKGOLON KYLON CQWRK

FLTTUG CNG LX KYG DOWVUGTNG KYCK SWR'UU

NBWV WRK WJ LK.   —TWBLX TCS

April 4

AS TEN AR OXLUG, H RTOAMHIG SHEMHRG LHE

MTMHOOG MIHERSTIP TEN PAOOATE

INHOAMANR.   —PHGH HEJNOTX

April 5

WORIR CRIR WHDRE DK LTPWE CRIR EN WOHP H

QNJSZ EHW NP T ZHDR TPZ WRSS HX HW CTE

ORTZE NI WTHSE.   —ELRPQRI WITQK

April 6

X QLUZ OQ X DHDLNA ALE TXU FOQBHU BL, X
DHDLNA TXMBENHW OU BKH FHXQB XDLEUB LR
CLNWQ.   —DHNFH KXZZXNW

April 7

KVTTOW OT DJX GHD VU TGCORK RVDJORK OR G
ZGC DJGD SXGQXT WHGBDOBGSSC RVDJORK
PRTGOF.   —ZGSDXH ZORBJXSS

April 8

H VCSR C TCLJVORY AVE JERD OE DIL. DVR
WELBT'SR JEGR OE LWBC, QLO HO'D EGR IEYR
BROORY DVR'T VCSR OE YRIRIQRY.

                                    —DVRWZN JYRRGR

April 9

M TMCD SDWS XRYXQR TDY DWIR AMZZMUHQSN
MF UYGGHFMUWSMFO TYHQA BHCS CDHS HX
WVYHS MS.   —SYG QRDPRP

··

April 10

D FDO'T XLFB FDE TBBF UL PB XHT VDTUIB LO

UXB LQUTHJB; HOTHJB, HU HT FLAB LGUBO XHT

OQATBAE.   —VIDAB PLLUXB IQVB

··

April 11

VKD YMEHV EDNCMEDODGV LY W HVWVDHOWG MH

VKWV KD AD FCZZ. VKMH MH GLV WZJWUH DWHU

VL WTKMDQD.   —FDWG WTKDHLG

··

April 12

LEPPDLL SL HBVHTL FDNGQCHCT. VJDR HBB SL

LHSY HRY YQRD, FJD QRBT FJSRZ TQE'BB JHXD

BDWF SL TQEC PJHCHPFDC.   —XSRPD ZSBB

··

April 13

CUV JYHC ASKPSXKV YG SKK CSKVZCH OH CUSC

YG ZVAVW PHOZB CQY QYWEH QUVZ YZV QOKK

EY.   —CUYJSH FVGGVWHYZ

33

April 14

C'D AY ECWWTXTAS WXYD JAMKYEM TRUT HCSP
SHY JXDU, SHY RTNU, JAE WYXSM-SHY PLAEXTE
PCSU.   —VTST XYUT

April 15

"GQBBYW PLAYWFMMF": AM BY AKMGY KPUY
PCHPRG JYYF AKY AHM BMGA JYPQANLQC HMWTG
NF AKY YFZCNGK CPFZQPZY.   —KYFWR VPBYG

April 16

CARKR TKR BZKR MTFUP WTJCG THP PRCTUFG UH
DZKXG ZW TKC CATH CARKR TKR UH AUGCZKI
LZZXG.   —JATKFUR JATQFUH

April 17

KDGRURFRTHV TML UAL VTBL LWLMNJALML.
UALN KMDBRVL UD ZXRGI ZMRIPLV LWLH JALML
UALML TML HD MRWLMV. —HRQRUT QAMXVAFALW

April 18

ALRT F AGW G JVC, F AGW SVOX SLGS GTCJVXC

IVZOX JRIVDR QMRWFXRTS; F'D JRKFTTFTK SV

JROFRYR FS.   —IOGMRTIR XGMMVA

··

April 19

CBLCOB XLTS KLFIZ NHB RSVHBXRJOP CLORIB.

BDBS IZBRH TNH TNK VRDRO.   —XFXOBP GLLHB

··

April 20

P'D CPLWY TN COPXQPXI P ORGW CT LPB DE

OWRLC TZC NTL WGWLE UORLRUCWL.

                              —AWFFPUR VRXIW

··

April 21

FYDO EHO HK DKUJPEYTHK'E YXTD PE YPE

MHEFJD. RYHF P RHKF PE FX FVWK TO MHEFJD

PKFX H YXTD.   —ZVDDK DJPLHCDFY PP

April 22

QVB MDT KV KUV HTVHMT DA QVBP MDGT: QVBP

LDPMGPDTAC JAC KWT HVMDYT. TXTPQVAT TMFT

QVB KTMM KWT KPBKW.   —ZJYN ADYWVMFVA

April 23

A FLJ IS L ZAPACU ZSUSCK, IXE EYLE GXDS

KNC'E YSZQ BYSC A'PS UNE EN VYLCUS L RZLE

EADS.   —DNJ NDIAGNC

April 24

SUF KFCS QPM SL ZFS URCKPAGC SL GL

PAMSUBAZ BC SL CRZZFCS SUPS JFVUPJC

SUFM'VF SLL LHG SL GL BS.

                             —CUBVHFM WPDHPBAF

April 25

G'D FS FUYHN, SHY F AYFN. AYFNA FNK

MKHMOK TZH OGJK GS ZHOOPTHHE FSE ZFJK

ZKFNY-AZFMKE ATGDDGSQ MHHOA. —FO MFUGSH

April 26

CQLORY Q MQMJ OV TOFW SQFORY JKHB TKPWB

TOD QRE AKBXORY OS KLWB JKHB CWQE.

—XQBKT MHBRWSS

April 27

L BXTJ TXRK SJT SPXYO. TXY TN SGYV LO

"KCXBYY ETTERY," CXE SGY TSGYQ LOX'S.

—PRKOOYO O. FQCXS

April 28

UT TRA FLYM GYUZR UD ORWWUTO ALYDR. U

AHD WBRYR WBR LWBRY PHF. WBR DWHWJR LN

CUSRYWF BHP SLWB BHTPD JV.   —KHF CRTL

April 29

NKCHZY YNIKBR NHEA SAHT IS SBPLZX QNA

YHCA DHP SLYN YNIKBR NHEA SAHT IS

RTLELZX.   —FATTP YALZSABR

N'T V FIGCMPA HICXKPNMBP VCS KB KPNMB

FPA-NC-AIGP-JBBP HICXH. MUVM'H KUVM KB

SI.   —KNZZNB CBZHIC

FB LIQE LVE LS VADI WQ, F CPXCED DCE, "F'JQ

SHPE TSL SHQ SLIQV DKQQY, CHY FL'D

DPSXQV."   —TPQHH BSVY

WCDND TND PUSR WHP WCXUBE T KCXSG HXSS

ECTND HXSSXUBSR—KPFFJUXKTVSD GXEDTEDE

TUG CXE FPWCDN'E TBD.   —VDUQTFXU EMPKZ

WHN TAS UK HUPS T FHTBS VHQUBA JOCWEAO T

KJWCX. WBZS QWE TCS TYWTCN JOSCS UK

BWJOUBA QWE ZTB NW.   —AWHNT XSUC

May 4

TEEJOWSS PEGOHARY JNR KECYJ TRWJZCRY ET

WGRCHPWA SHTR—TCWAJHP BHESRAPR

DZAPJZWJRI OF PEGGHJJRR GRRJHAVY.

—VRECVR KHSS

May 5

V CRUVRER FWLF VQ RERG V WLY FB ZGLKFVKR

KLPPVCLUVXJ, V JVIWF JLPLIR VQ FWRGR ORGR

RPBAIW FLGGLIBP LGBAPY. —NLJRX CRLGY

May 6

GBPY ZMA'VP CMGY WYC MAF, NMOPFBHYD

WTGWZN FAVYN AL—WYC HF'N ANAWTTZ FBP

YMNPN MQ ZMAV QVHPYCN. —MVNMY GPTTPN

May 7

P WTKER BMZL CEMNLR JHT TF JBFLL GTFL

NLMFD. MEE P XLLRLR HMD M ELY JFMXDCEMXJ.

—QTBXXN KXPJMD

39

May 8

GL'E J FVMVEEGHS TAVS ZHDF SVGYAKHF PHEVE

AGE CHK; GL'E J RVBFVEEGHS TAVS ZHD PHEV

ZHDF HTS.   —AJFFZ E LFDXJS

May 9

SCHE EBGO JHM THIK GCY YH EBGO JHM THIK.

PZ JHM YHC'O YH EBGO JHM THIK, JHM'VK

WMNO EGNOPCX JHMV OPDK.   —FPTTJ WHKT

May 10

MZ JKE'VS HVMGMAX UKAXU, GFSVS TVS GHK

GFMAXU GFTG JKE REUG CKA'G HVMGS TLKEG:

BKQMGMNU TAC VSQMXMKA. HS HVMGS TLKEG

LKGF.   —LKAK

May 11

WANPN'C ZM NUNVNMW BR WPGWA JM NHNPF

JSNZ WAZW UZCWC UBMY NMBGYA WB QN

LZUUNS LBPMF.   —JPHJMY QNPUJM

HFCS OWDXDSK, PSTYUOT KUDSK JIUHCW LFPS

TUZ DJ PS DODUL, PSO PSTYUOT KUDSK VPJLCW

LFPS TUZ DJ P BUWUS.   —KCUWKC MPWIDS

DTLDOT GS KWALLO SLOF JT H WLVOFQ'S

JGPT HS, SAGS H CLVOF TQF VD JGPHQZ

DLSALOFTXK.   —KSTBHT CLQFTX

BPY DYBBYG BPY LMKOYG'L AQMNY, BPY PHGXYG

MB ML BQ DYZMYAY CPHB BPYE'GY LHEMKO, LQ

M FLYX JE VHFZBL BQ HK HXAHKBHOY.

—XHAMX DEGKY

KG TED MEDFW EF R WEEN YRNW LFEDOY, SEFO

LFEDOY, EGILF LFEDOY, PEEFLN EN SRILN

PEALVEWT HKSS EMLF KI.   —ZYRBB MRSAKFILNK

··

May 16

BIM CH ZROX ISLIWTIDOI CH JGR OCD, HG MXCM

JGR'WI WICUJ QXID PRON QGWNH. MXCM'H MXI

PRON. —XIDWJ VGDUC

··

May 17

PHL EH HGD MRE OBCGK R PDRJ RGE CO KDOI

ORFADE RMHLO NHJ OBD JDIO HN PHLJ FCND.

—EDMJR ZCGKDJ

··

May 18

OVG OVLCAT FCG TSET SWG SHH BCTBMMGTTDBH

SOOGYJOT OF TSE TFYGOVLCA GHTG.

—KGWOWSCI WBTTGHH

··

May 19

HBW FPAV RPVEWLG AV HBAG DAKW PLW HBW

ZWUZDW TBU TPVH HU QBPVEW WOWLXHBAVE ...

UL VUHBAVE. —VPVQX PGHUL

May 20

JBIBEPHPGK PH JUB FPKC GY JUPKW TGD SMT

MJJBKJPGK JG PY TGD VPHU, MKC PY TGD

CGK'J, TGD WG JG LIBMK GDJ TGDA CAMVBAH.

—LUBA

May 21

DGOP THR DHFS AOXOP YMTA M DOOS,

JHRFEOOP GHRFA M YMT, THR BOE WRNST.

—MFLMPY GMLLOF

May 22

PLFCVAKCRH GEVBX EVRDCEM DCMDLK RDYE

CRXLZS, TNR RYZLER CEXRYERZH KLAVMECILX

MLECNX.   —YKRDNK AVEYE FVHZL

May 23

FMB ACYGUBK ZJFM GBDLFS JP FMDF JF'P UJVB

GBJWR GYCW CJXM DWQ RBFFJWR AYYCBC.

—HYDW XYUUJWP

43

May 24

CSTMTETY A STXY XRJFN XMJNSTY TDEAL
LAPSNAMP, AN PAETL HT X STXZXBST.

—GYALBADDX GYTLDTU

May 25

I ALFY BO TY JFIELF MAIT IT YFQBTIFS KIT,
JHM AL BO JFIEL GBEL KBTHMLO CYTDLF.

—FICZA PICQY LKLFOYT

May 26

SIGILK NOIFUL DIBR AI AOR BIJZRN FSURNN OR
GRUZRJRN ZS ORVIRN.   —MIOS PTKSR

May 27

BOM APZM BOPAX RVLEB VMPAX R ZMWMVYPBN
PD BORB PT NLE VLYM QMLQWM BOMN BOPAC
PB'D BOMPY TREWB.   —OMAYN CPDDPAXMY

May 28

GTKI GCBBJCURK WTE'I CWW IHT FRTFXR

ITURIDRB. IDRN KOSIBCLI TER PBTG IDR

TIDRB.   —JCE PXRGJEU

May 29

TWEG IR P IPH GWE KBPZT P VEEF VPIR EA

VEBA, PHF C'BB TWEG ZEJ P IPH GWE'T

HRVBRONCHV TEIRNWCHV.   —MEWH A. YRHHRFZ

May 30

ZINOL TOOM K YMOFPKX FIDLOD IR SWOPD

WOKDSY RID YPLY SWOH WKGO LOGOD

FINNPSSOE.   —FIDLOXPK ISPY YTPLLOD

May 31

DOY DWPHMSY FQDO TPCD PL HC QC DOVD FY

FPHSG WVDOYW MY WHQEYG MX ZWVQCY DOVE

CVKYG MX JWQDQJQCT.—EPWTVE KQEJYED ZYVSY

June 1

PLAATZLLK'F J WAJHO ZPODO GPOT'AA WJT TLR

J GPLRFJVK KLAAJDF ELD J MXFF JVK EXEGT

HOVGF ELD TLRD FLRA.   —BJDXATV BLVDLO

••

June 2

OFSPS BN V WLLZ ZSVY OLL NOPVAWS OL GS

GSYBSMSZ; ALOFBAW BN OLL NOPVAWS OL FVMS

FVTTSASZ.   —OFLQVN FVPZX

••

June 3

AR FIDQ MIAVE IR YALK AN QAJOE, FIDQ

HSSDQL KASS EHZL BHQL IR AENLSR.

—MHDSLEEL JITTHQT

••

June 4

CVTUP BHN B UBHK TC VZCN'P FNAX BAJ Z'LN

ANLNH SNNA B WZHV KT FZPP TXK TA BAD TC

KIN GTXHPNP.   —HTPBVZAJ HXPPNVV

June 5

OKGXG GSAG DY AHZDGPF MH FHB KUCG PKG

SDZGYAG PH GUCGAMXHL HY AH NUYF

MDRRGXGYP ZHYCGXAUPDHYA UA FHB KUCG DY

VHBXYUSDAN?   —WDSS NHFGXA

June 6

BN WME LHF UMGGFGGFY ZW LD BYFL, WME

NBDY BK FRUHFGGFY FAFHWQTFHF—WME FAFD

GPFSS BK.   —KTMPLG PLDD

June 7

GWOK HYE PAH RHY TZD TOK PATE RHY IETOK

GHZ, TOK CDTZO EAD KWGGDZDOJD XDEPDDO

ZWQAE TOK PZHOQ; XD TXCD EH PDWQA

EAWOQI.   —BZWOJD

June 8

H PTOD PSELDKSQB! FSE WTBD OPD VDUL, FSE

US OPD UHLPDL—TJU LHG WSJOPL ZTODQ FSE

PTND OS LOTQO TZZ SNDQ TYTHJ.

                              —MSTJ QHNDQL

47

··

June 9

A DMEV DT COLREN JRKMXLR A EAVR ZRMEAYS
FADP M JRDDRW KEMLL TN GRTGER.

—BMKVAR CMLTY

··

June 10

BVIT X GXT DCITA WVI RXE UDDE NDE VHA
BHNI, HW'A IHWVIE X TIB RXE DE X TIB BHNI.

—CEHTRI CVHYHC

··

June 11

G FHPEES COBPELB REEBNGSS OF OT QGTYMD ER
QMBMDOEDGBOTY OTBE G XMQOMJGS FBLQK
PGSS.   —JOTHM SEXNGDQO

··

June 12

JW'A DZDNJFB XTC ZDFP HGTHQG KGDW PTR
DW BTQM FTC WXDW PTR'VG FT QTFBGV
HVGAJEGFW.   —BGTVBG KRAX

June 13

K'AT BTTX JEVTX KX CUVB JNE VHBD MT
JEFQKXC EHD BEVTJNTFT TOBT DE OEEQ CEEZ
TXEHCN DE LEVT DE DNT CUV.   —DKV YOOTX

June 14

CRYCKR UHL OYE HKJHLA EPMOD TMZ
EPRUARKXRA, TGE EPRL VHO AEMKK ZRE XRBL
RQVMERS TL EPYAR JPY SY.   —SYOHKS EBGUC

June 15

LM BYFTYOVZ OZ THMWXA, CDW LIMZ LM'XM
MJMBWMS, LM'XM GHXBMS WH VHPMXZ OZ
TXHKM.   —FYXOH BDHFH

June 16

NFGL MHZL PHVLY BGALNMS, QANEHGN JDKKLFY
HF RMDYEAKT MATENY. AR SHG ELDF JLMMY,
TLN SHGF LDFY PELPOLX.   —LFAPE YLTDM

June 17

BROZLIDI IZHCE CLCHDG ZHOQHCD TV DBHLO

MLFHI DNCLCY DBHLO BROZI RCE DHC ZHOQHCD

ZMRGLCY TND TV DNCH.   —LYTO IDORFLCIXG

June 18

WM'B THHK MH TH MH MPF CHZWFB JQHXF

DFYJRBF HXYF LHR TFM MPFVF, LHR'VF XHM

JQHXF. LHR'VF JM MPF CHZWFB. —VHTFV FDFVM

June 19

PHGO H PHG FDUCLU CL FLAL UBARGI LGRMIC

BR BLHA H BLWLSCRGL VRRY DG CHWX—

LUSLTDHWWO DX CL CHU H BLLGHIL NHMICBLA.

                              —IMO WRPVHANR

June 20

BTL WROGNY TPI PGJPDI LMWLYBLE CL BF OL P

WGPDOFD, PKE P ELYLKB YTPW KLALH GLBI TNI

WROGNY EFJK.   —LHHFG ZGDKK

June 21

ZOFSS H'PUHPQ BD KUJKMD ZHH UKZS HF ZHH

SKFUM AHF KYMZOBYC MHR JKYZ ZH GH.

—LSKY-VKRU DKFZFS

June 22

GAOHKY PM SUY VHZF KVEHSAF CUYAY SUY

BVHYF GOZZM OTOAS OHQ FVE KOH'S SYOA SUY

SVPZYS TOTYA.   —JPZZF CPZQYA

June 23

WZ GHD IHK'S UWBN CHVNSTWKR OYHDS

GHDFCNUZ, LTOKRN WS. WZ GHD LOK'S LTOKRN

WS, OLLNXS WS.   —SNI CTOLBNUZHFI

June 24

CRNPO GDNX TYJ PHN PXIHT PXE TYJ GBFF

VPON ZDN WNCZ CRNNQD TYJ GBFF NANH

HNIHNZ.   —PVWHYCN WBNHQN

June 25

DFOTMBTNHDLGE BJ TYSE OT MR OHFJORK IGRY
BO HRPRDSJ JTVROGBYN KBJNHDZRXFS.

—NRTHNR THIRSS

June 26

GLP NXCUK YX UXG ZUXR PUXCKL GX AP
EICYPUG, MUY GLPIPDXIP GLPN MGGPJEG GLP
QJEXWWQABP—MUY MTLQPOP QG. —EPMIB ACTZ

June 27

CBS HGCANALC AL KYC CBS FHK PBY LHML CBS
DANSD AL JADCM. CBS HGCANALC AL CBS FHK
PBY GXSHKL QV CBS DANSD. —DYLL VSDYC

June 28

FI CRHY FI KEN ZRACG TNNMI KOAHLHY FHG
IMLHHLHY, ZN'AN YRHHF VN GLPPS, FHG ZN'AN
YRHHF QFTN QLIKFTNI. —QNC VARRTI

June 29

BXDM PHR'VD FM GHKD FJ'O JXD CHOJ

EGHVFHRO JBH-ZMT-Z-XZGL TZPO HL PHRV

GFLD.   —VFQXZVT GDBFO

June 30

RTDL HOAH DS W ENWVE LN GN, KH D VJBOHDC

ABWHVLWAL? DOO W PVNR TNR LN GN WA

MWETL.   —SWPH LUANV

July 1

TNF WSDM GN WSDM JVMSG ZSYL SLE

FLWSZZYLMOO—NGWMVCYOM, WNC CNFPE TNF

XLNC CWML TNF'VM WSZZT?   —PMOPYM BSVNL

July 2

ERIBG TNY CRLB ERLS CLBE ERANVTR OS

PHNDLED ERLS WNVBY DRNLD, BNE DGLHLENBD.

—JOLHYI OIAPND

July 3

WJSLS OT M ILSSP EN NMTJOEG KEPSRT AJE

ASOUJ GE KELS WJMG MG MILOPUSP

POFWOEGMLD. —PMZS IMLLD

July 4

FHR FU IKR DRXI TMNX IF BRMXJAR GRFGQR

OX IF TMILK IKR TMN IKRN DRKMER TKRH

XFBRIKOHY UARR OX FUURARC. —MHH QMHCRAX

July 5

XAZ BEZUXZNX PUNXZECOZHZ OY MOXZEUXFEZ

ON TYMS U KOHXOTYUES TFX TQ TEKZE.

—DZUY HTHXZUF

July 6

R CHARB OT WOSK R YKR JRM; QHF BKIKP SBHC

EHC TYPHBM TEK OT FBYOW TEK MKYT OB EHY

CRYKP. —BRBGQ PKRMRB

July 7

O QCXCJ DYJCG KQ OSSCFKS ZODBY. DYC
DJTHISC OM, TQBC OQ K GYOSC O DTMM TQC
DYKD KOQ'D QCXCJ ICCQ MCCQ IP DYOM
FCQCJKDOTQ.   —MKDBYCS ZKOFC

July 8

FNNG TJHJFWTWHM ANHELEME NR ECNVLHF
JIWOJFW QWNQZW CNV MN GN MCW VNOD NR
EKQWOLNO QWNQZW.   —BNCH G. ONADWRWZZWO

July 9

CROG DYE TOA MKIA NVNAD, DYE RKJO AY
BOLVBO CROAROP AY WOOM DYEP NKLO YP DYEP
NVTEPO. V WOMA UD NKLO.

                              —ZKPZKPK LKPAHKGB

July 10

KGEKSG QJUY CE SGNDH CE UQJA NHW NC CYG
UNAG CJAG CE LGGK EHG BEEC EH CYG FDEXHW.

                              —ANDVGS KDEXUC

July 11

B YIGR T PGS GJ OHGOPH SWBIY B'D VADN.

RHPP, TS PHTKS B TBI'S IG HVALTSHV JGGP.

—PHGI KOBIYK

July 12

R WAK'S BKAX SCY BYE SA NHPPYNN, JHS SCY

BYE SA GORTHMY RN SMERKZ SA FTYONY

YQYMEJAWE. —JRTT PANJE

July 13

J WUH'B VTF SHZ DFBGUW. J'D KEUD BGF

"XFB'T QEFBFHW" TPGUUX UK SPBJHL.

—GSEEJTUH KUEW

July 14

BD CTYOS KOLF NR EMOAWY OY ANE EN MTKL

TAD CTYOS KOLF NR EMOAWY.

—OAWBTH CLHWBTA

July 15

GL'Y POO IGMVL LD VDOF P UDZAKIYPLGDZ, JBL

QDB YVDBOF OKL MD DX GL ZDE PZF LVKZ.

—IGUVPIF PICDBI

July 16

HEZY CHS LZSLMZ MSBZ ZTOE SCEZG, CEZR

WSY'C MSSP TC ZTOE SCEZG, CEZR MSSP DY CEZ

FTXZ WDGZOCDSY.   —KDYKZG GSKZGF

July 17

FUVE B DS AS AUV WVCXAR JCMTSM, B CTFCRN

XNV AUV VGVMDVEQR VEAMCEQV. NSGVABGVN B

ZXNA DS YSM CE VNABGCAV. —JURTTBN KBTTVM

July 18

BX N ENL'T RINANRWKA BT WH OK NODTKG, TNP

JINW PHD JBZZ, WIKAK'T LHOHGP ZBQK N

AKZNWBHL WH GH WIK ODTBLKTT.

—JBZZBNE WINRQKANP

57

July 19

DLOGEOGY OT VLTF RBVG FHN CHG'E JGHR BHR,

ZNE QVXF COMMOPNSE RBVG FHN CH.

—VCYLX CVYLT

July 20

JIF EBUH JARF P CERPB WFPUUH DMLLFFXD AB

LIPBVABV P RPB AD CIFB IF'D P ZPZH.

—BPJPUAF CEEX

July 21

JAFY UN PGBFD UN JAFY TGL HOOD VGGE

FHYOB, FME JAFY UN UPPGBFD UN JAFY TGL

HOOD SFE FHYOB.   —OBMONY AOPUMVJFT

July 22

GR YEM KLL GD PULDMN, PLIM LWMQ YL YEM

DMBXYM. TLC'UU HMY YEM DXIM FGBN LR

RMMUGBH XBN TLC VLB'Y EXWM YL JXT.

—SLS NLUM

July 23

DWSFF MF BF SOBVPUBZS B HBFZS PK WLQBE

MEZSOOMRSEDS BF TPL DBE KMEY PLZFMYS BE

BYJSUZMFMER BRSEDT.   —UBTQPEY DWBEYOSU

July 24

SNTOY TPRE EHK EN GN EFBYUR MR TOY FMZO

EHBOG. SFOY EFOK QMBD, EFOBH QMBDPHO

TPRE AO APE M WFMDDOYUO EN NEFOHR.

—MTODBM OMHFMHE

July 25

JRE'S HRDULS ZPRXS GRXDBLOH ZEJ ZOO RH Z

BXJJLE PLWRAL CQZS RSQLD VLRVOL BLL GRX

ZB—BRALREL'B DLOZSYKL.   —DRULD WOYESRE

July 26

T'M OTPH CE LESH WBLP BN BV EFNCHY. CZHV

T'M EVOF ZBQH CE WH KEEM JYES NHACHSWHY

XVCTO BAYTO.   —KYBLTH BOOHV

59

July 27

R WLF'U PHFU UL HTIRMZM ROOLBUHDRUE NE
OHCRFS UIM IHDD LA AHOM. R PHFU UL
HTIRMZM ROOLBUHDRUE NE FLU WERFS.

— DML WGBLTIMB

July 28

GING'D CMP CU GIP GKNYPBLPD CU GILD ALUP,
GING GIP VPM TIC NKP VCDG LM MPPB CU N
HPNGLMY JQ NKP NATNFD PMCKVCJD.

— KJBF SNAAPP

July 29

RWOOGAR FGLFWY TDO TK OVW BPWXGLBA JBX
BNNTLGBOGTA GN HGFW RWOOGAR FGLFWY TDO
TK OVW JTTF-TK-OVW-PTAOV LHDJ.

— PWHZGA JWHHG

July 30

KEL BLOHLK JG CPUPXQUX QB KJ DLLM KEL
XZAB TEJ EPKL AJZ PTPA GHJC KEL JULB TEJ
PHL ZURLOQRLR.   — OPBLA BKLUXLN

60

July 31

DMYOOYG RO BY ABE YCFYNSO LE PWISRSXGY,

TEW BY OBIMM LES DY GROIFFERLSYG.

—ARMMRIZ DYLLYSS

August 1

CVNCS BY YWUDCSBGP TWN YCNUFHD BGCW ZSDG

TWN CSBGQ TWN'VD PWBGP YWUDJHLXD DHYD.

—KDVVT PLVXBL

August 2

QRGFIXOM RPDO MODOX AOOM DOXT ZWWI PN

FGVNOMGMZ NW NROGX OFIOXV, AHN NROT RPDO

MODOX BPGFOI NW GYGNPNO NROY.

—KPYOV APFIJGM

August 3

S GKMY NTY JTHGGYURY KW BNHDNSUR HN FYDK

YHJT EHQ HUE BYYSUR TKZ IPJT S JHU

HJJKICGSBT. —IHDNTH BNYZHDN

······································

August 4

FULMIR PHNMD MAL CLHP NIUG MAL AHTTLY

JLXEMR UN MAL KUIPT.

— FLIZR JRDDAL DALPPLR

······································

August 5

ZPLSLZH BJMO ROMOP FOOR JFXO SN WLHZNMOP

J KRLTVLRD SBOQO LR QV TLXQH. TNP SBJS

QJSSOP, ROLSBOP BJMO L.   — YNBR BKHSNR

······································

August 6

YOP NPALPY CX NYHSVFE SCMFE VN YC TVKP

OCFPNYTS, PHY NTCZTS, HFQ TVP HWCMY SCML

HEP.   — TMAVTTP WHTT

······································

August 7

COZ OMPOFMPOC TQ SJ BOMFYOTTY ERD SRWMUP

SJ ANTCOZN FRHPO DT ORNY CORC QTTY BRSZ

THC TQ OMD UTDZ.   — PRNNMDTU WZMFFTN

2

August 8

O SLYOSLS MP GLYPWL TZ TYMPH GLYTVEL O

ATE JTOXOZI OZ EYDPPX TZS O ZLLSLS MDL

YHLSOME.   —SVEMOZ DPJJWTZ

August 9

GP HYL DAKE HCRA G LPYWPRZ PD LCYNR BE

CRYZ YAZ ZWRLL ZGMMRWRAPKE PCYP G

WRYKGSRZ G CYZ Y NDGTR YL PD HCD G HYL.

                              —JGKKGYA YAZRWLDA

August 10

PSUDDUJ TEU GLU NCIWK, ACE GLUN DLTSS

HWLUEHG GLU WTGHCWTS JUPG.

                              —LUEPUEG LCCZUE

August 11

JRADY KRORLSRK AN HOSRD L SRVTHELEX

QHDKASAHD. YABADY FT AN CULS VLWRN AS

TREVLDRDS.   —VLEAZXD BHN NLBLDS

August 12

QAT KHG QP CHET H JBUC BN QP ZTVBY KBQA

HY THOQADMHET HYX KPOE MR QP H FUBCHW.

—FTFBU Z. XTCBUUT

August 13

SAHDU "HYD JBQSUE FA FQ" B JSN HLRDKSNH

SN S OBFX, SXE HYDUD SUDX'H SOO HYSH ZSXL

RSUHN AFU OBFXN. —GDUH OSYU

August 14

JUCH TNI VAIZT RUMKNVNRUT MH VWUNNK, TNI

ECLCLXCE BIVA CHNIQU AN VWECJ TNI IR SNE

AUC ECVA NS TNIE KMSC. —VACYC LFEAMH

August 15

G YSJD IFHBZOD QGIY IHSNI. IHSNI GN JDFM

RGWWGXBOI. MHB YSJD IH QSIXY GI SOO IYD

IGKD HF GI ZBFPN BV. —LBOGS XYGOR

August 16

A EBUECN JEVR FXR UHDNF-SDRNNRS BANF. AF

AN VATS HY TAZR XEWATK NHJRFXATK CHG ZET

ZHGTF HT. —JESHTTE

August 17

OUPY GUDDJTYS QPROPPY ROD PLTZJ, T HZOHMJ

ZTEP RD RHEP RUP DYP T'LP YPLPV RVTPF

QPXDVP. —WHP OPJR

August 18

CB VKPPERKKM, TPP UTFFCTYHW TFH VTNNE.

CG'W GFECBY GK PCZH GKYHGVHF TJGHFRTFM

GVTG STLWHW GVH NFKXPHUW.

—WVHPPHE RCBGHFW

August 19

ZOLLFT PHT OQ CUTX KWD'RT ZTE QW ZPXK

BTWBFT EUPE TRTJK XTC BTJQWX KWD ZTTE

JTZOXLQ KWD WS QWZTWXT TFQT.

—WHLTX XPQU

August 20

L EHUX PZ JX CUXHP. PVX YHB KLPVZQP

LYHCLBHPLZB APHBEA QBVQUP HBE VHA BZ

KLBCA.   —EZB WLBC

August 21

L ZDDB ADG WDQFW HEPH WPS JEPH VMVGS XPQ

JDRZK ZLBV HD YV PYZV HD WPS, PQK VMVGS

JDXPQ JDRZK ZLBV HD EVPG.   —BVQQS GDFVGW

August 22

NZC WZT'H EBIR HZ GCAT GZZPQ HZ WRQHAZN B

VCXHCAR. DCQH MRH FRZFXR HZ QHZF ARBWJTM

HERK.   —ABN GABWGCAN

August 23

MUB FLOBAMOXOL MUBJIG O POVB ZBFM OF

MUKM MUB IOASF JX FKMYIA KIB LJCWJFBR

BAMOIBPG JX PJFM KOIPOAB PYSSKSB.

                                        —CKIV IYFFBPP

66

August 24

W CELO W OSQ FYBOE HG OZLE W YSE JSVC

WEAB BHY JHYELI-BHA ZBHQL AB GHA BE

DSCL-HG TBY AZL VHAL TWYLDLE.

—DSYXLL DSAXWE

August 25

PAHCHIM TWQXC ZXOHU HO FHVD GTIUHIM

TWQXC TAULHCDUCXAD—HC'O T ADTFFN OCXYHG

CLHIM CQ PTIC CQ GQ.   —DFKHO UQOCDFFQ

August 26

H LUGFFYTGPKFG PL H WHY TBR PL MFPYO

KRGKZGFE KR URYVFLL HYE BHL YRKBPYO KR

URYVFLL.   —UBGPLKRIBFG PLBFGTRRE

August 27

G WAS'H JUSH USP PCI-QCS UVAFSW QC. G JUSH

CNCVPTAWP HA HCDD QC HOC HVFHO CNCS GK

GH LAIHI HOCQ HOCGV MATI. —IUQFCD ZADWJPS

67

··

August 28

PHR HRURX SPRL LP TFX FL KERH PHR CPRLH'D
YHPK KERXR PHR NL SPNHS.

—WPEFHH KPATSFHS UPH SPRDER

··

August 29

L CBHOVG'S MTAR OLARV JE OLXR SMR CTE L
VLV LX L CTZ DBLGD SB CBPPE TQBHS CMTS
KRBKOR CRPR DBLGD SB ZTE. — LGDPLV QRPDJTG

··

August 30

SFF H GSEW QLW QB FHBP HJ WASW GAPE H
GSFX VQGE WAP JWIPPW, BQFXJ GHFF JSU,
"WAPIP NQPJ WAP NIPSWPJW AHWWPI GAQ PDPI
FHDPV." —WPV GHFFHSYJ

··

August 31

Z'L DNGSU PG FC DYHZIX PYJCV ZI PQC SIZPCU
VPYPCV. PQC GIKH PQZIX ZV, Z WGSKU FC YV
DNGSU TGN QYKT PQC LGICH.

—YNPQSN XGUTNCH

68

September 1

V TGMME CALC CAS FSMBGW TAG CAGNPAC NF

QNYLJ QLE DS CAVWJVWP NF BGQSCAVWP SHBS.

—HVHE CGQHVW

September 2

W'P F PLFSALFJ. W VFM'S ALUB WS, PFM.

DKH'RL NKS ZPFCS BLKBUL FMJ DKH'RL NKS

JHPX BLKBUL. —ELFMH CLLRLZ

September 3

NX RSKOWSJ JOOK ND SLL NOE ZDHELJ ND KO,

JD A KSTO AN S ZDFARG EOXOW ND OSN NX

RSKOWSJ. —TANNG RSWFAJFO

September 4

DB VDPTF ADYT VQTFT, DV QTACF VJ XTKWAA

VQWV VQTXT QWET WAGWHF STTB VDPTF ADYT

VQTFT. —CWRA QWXETH

September 5

L SNGGTETNR TE HILC ILKKPRE HIPR CHN

DNCNJTECE BN LQCPJ CIP ELDP KPOPECJTLR.

—MNM RPHILJC

September 6

NOLULXLB JDC'BL GEWWEUZ PRBDGG QBDK GDKL

EKFDBWPUW FLBGDU, PHNPJG FERWCBL OEK

GEWWEUZ WOLBL EU P GCEW DQ HDUZ BLA

CUALBNLPB.   —SDGLFO TLUULAJ

September 7

DR TLP BGN LSMGY, TLP MHB MGGFGY HONL

NKG ZYGDNHCG JGSS NL WHOM LPN JKDN NKG

YGDS RLPYZG HR.   —ZKYHRRHG KTOMG

September 8

CMP CAVLOZP YGCM CPZZGIF S FVVX HCVAB GH

CMSC GC GIJSAGSOZB APKGIXH CMP VCMPA

UPZZVY VU S OSX VIP.   —HGX QSPHSA

70

....

September 9

ADESNHDWIE WHY GDPY MYWL CYNCGY TAN RN

NI WIETYHDIR FBYESDNIE SAWS IN NIY AWE

WEPYM SAYO.   —GYN SNGESNQ

....

September 10

H OSPN S DHJ DOSD USK DSAN LHPN MDETANM

TLL SKRTKN'M VTWL VSIN: HD'M USWWNZ SK

NESMNE.   —SEKTWZ JSWINE

....

September 11

CQCUD FLW H PHUC HE GUHAPICU IPLW FC.

LVICU LZZ, HV H'F LE EFLUI LE DXJ LUC, H

KXW'I WCCK DXJ.   —GCLU GUDLWI

....

September 12

WHAN H WHA IHU CHDDRA OA DSQR JOEI H

ZOBD OA H DOZIE US TOW IR JSPDT ASE IHQR

FISURA H UPOE MN OE.   —WHPBOFR FIRQHDORB

September 13

AN AD CPH JZHW AJYHWDDAGW BEWL ZNEWHD

MADTZGWH RZFH SZZM KFPQANAWD BANEZFN

RZFH EWQY.   —OFMANE JPHNAL

September 14

L KUGUB ZHKSUX ST QU H MDFFUMM, PTB SAU

GUBR JTTX BUHMTK SAHS LP L ZUBUK'S H

MDFFUMM, L ZTDWX QU DKAHNNR. —MHY KULWW

September 15

TF TUQPTBLMLKAGY AG YPB JBGY PRGJTFX TFD

ZLOTF QTF PTCB; YPB LMXBU GPB KBYG, YPB

OLUB AFYBUBGYBX PB AG AF PBU.

                              —TKTYPT QPUAGYAB

September 16

TN OS TLD, A EKZS HDODOWDH NRE NJAKLX:

ZTUADX THD VHDNNS TKU OEKDS VTSX NJD

WAZZX AB SEP FTK LDN AN.   —W.W. MAKL

September 17

L FLVB UBLSZ X PXHRDN CELOBE. AERUFBH LN,

BQBET RSIB LS X CGLFB TRD GXQB OR CELOB

NRHBOGLSZ.   —VBS VBNBT

September 18

T GOGORVBH PALOFS VB JBFF PFKGBS, SHBPPBS

JKCA DBDDBH TXS MKXBNTH, TXS CABX CAHLJX

LOC.   —PTROBF YLAXPLX

September 19

NW PCH'RM FCD CIM FCCY BNGMV AZEYM,

PCH'VM NI FCCY KLEGM—EK ZCIF EK ND'K CI

DLM YVNRMV'K KNYM.   —DVNKLE PMEVBCCY

September 20

TLQ MBBLMD CT ZCZEF BLJULHE YIME FVK'RL

PVE MHW ZCZEF BLJULHE YIME BLVBDL EICHG

FVK'RL PVE.   —TVBICM DVJLH

September 21

TAWP AN TF RAJODW ZIJO SOOR UDIGR

NGYPGAR NAB UDIGR NADMW, PZO DGPOBIBF

OKQGJIDORP AN I SGL TIY IRE DIBLO NBGOW.

—WPOUZOR MGRL

September 22

FTOQCHM TRAXF PAXY FYAXRODU CU HA MAAW.

DCMEFP BDYLDHF AJ PAXY JYCDHWU WAH'F LTYD

THW FED YDUF TYD MOTW.   —FAZZP OTUAYWT

September 23

WHE JMPUB UQB DHYS FEDU VHM WHEMDBCV,

TEU PU'D YH SHHO EYCBDD WHE ACZW PU VHM

DHXBTHOW BCDB.   —TMEKB DAMPYSDUBBY

September 24

CHP WHE'X FBOXY ZYLTPGY CHP FTEX XH GTC

GHQYXKOEV; CHP FBOXY ZYLTPGY CHP'RY VHX

GHQYXKOEV XH GTC.   —J. GLHXX JOXAVYBTDW

September 25

FCRY ZM FRZMRAM YCR AMXMU JRFFGBF, LAT
G'KK FCRY SRN FRZMRAM YCR GFA'H
GAHMUMFHMT GA BMRBKM. —VLUVLUL YLKHMUF

September 26

P CROD DUDBGPLD. OH LRT THN KDO NZ RO
QHNB H'GEHGF PI OCD WHBIPIK RIS EPFD OH
DUDBGPLD, THN'S YD ZLTGCHOPG.

—MRGF ERERIID

September 27

JRGZRKEONT OGGOEBERL BL HRSS BL OE
BEEGBKEL, OT ZOKEONT BL OT SOZR.

—SNMOL BMKYOTKSNLL

September 28

GMFECGHE GCE KF G OCRXSHE RY ETB
SPEGUBPEBX FRUX MN ETB SPOCKPHKOUBX ER
ETB SEEBCUN MBJKUXBCBX.   —GU HGOO

September 29

BZ'G ZLP WRON FPDFWP SLD BMXPMZPA ZLP

SLPPW RMA ZLP JBYNYWP JPYRIGP ZLPN ABAM'Z

WBTP SRWTBME DV YRVVNBME ZLBMEG.

—WPYL SRWPGR

September 30

G'LY MAPUA BRR TF RGDY G VPNRO QBMY B

SNAVK PD UPJOX BAO QKJPU QKYT NZ GA QKY

BGJ BAO QKYF UPNRO VPTY OPUA CNXQ JGEKQ.

—QJNTBA VBZPQY

October 1

VN PAWSAH QMDL VL BFO VAGSJB SA YFDL, KCS

ZJLG F WACYPG'S RMN SJL KFYY, JL QMDL VL

BFO VAGSJB VAHL.   —ZMYSLH VMSSJMC

October 2

OHY MF END O QOVDMAXGOVGT MEDYVVYFDMEH

FXZWYAD. OETNEY AOE HYD NGU. OGG TNX KOPY

DN UN MF GMPY GNEH YENXHK. —HVNXAKN LOVI

October 3

GYFT RT CGB YVBMNOYW DBRDFB WBPBM

MBYQ Y WBHIDYDBM. GYFT WBPBM PRCB TRM

DMBINQBWC. RWB GRDBI NC NI CGB IYVB GYFT.

—KRMB PNQYF

October 4

JK PHR YLLE D VLJAJYO BDJYWLE, D VCDFJHW

FDVL FRY, D VJWP QLTJLOLE, HF WCL FLE TLD

BDFWLE, PHR WCJYG HK IL. —VCDFAWHY CLTWHY

October 5

WU'B VRBH UF MRIV JOWYKWJGVB TMVY HFP'OV

OWKM. UMV WQJFOURYU UMWYN WB UF MRIV

JOWYKWJGVB TMVY HFP'OV JFFO.   —ORH DOFK

October 6

GLDDNFLLZ OX FGUMU YGUN FMOYU YGU CDOJOX

JUKLMU YGUN FMOYU YGU XYLMN.

—PCMLDU DLSJCMZ

October 7

HE LSKLZX MN H CHE TRD RHN CHJL HOO XRL

CMNXHVLN TRMGR GHE IL CHJL ME H WLZF

EHZZDT YMLOJ.   —EMLON IDRZ

October 8

G PREGRWR SZLS FGOK LK TREE LK LOJESK LHR

RCSGSERO SN PNNFK NX CN KNMGLEEA

HRORRVGCY WLEJR.   —H.E. KSGCR

October 9

TIMS G TBC B ZMBEQM, G EIPNJIE TM TMLM EIM

ZMCE JLPNK GS EIM TPLQH, BSH ZMQGMWGSJ

EIBE GC TIBE OBHM NC TIBE TM TMLM.

—UPIS QMSSPS

October 10

JGT FDFTKJ DV RQXJDBM QO FWXG JDD OGDBJ

JD UQRT VDB JGPJ PKY KDJGQKZ TUOT.

—FPBJQKP KPRBPJQUDRP

78

October 11

P TWUH FOHIK BWIJ JHWDF RZ BJ VPZH PI

ROORFPKPRI WIE P DWKTHD VPMH KTH DRVH.

—HVHWIRD DRRFHUHVK

October 12

RIWDNAWDR HCDL A RFDTZ A RTE "HD,"

QDGTJRD A WDTL WD TLX WE OIAGD. HD TMD

NHI XAPPDMDLN NCALKR. —BJGATLI FTOTMINNA

October 13

FUMPYZPB ZP USH JZYYOH LK USH XLMY ZF

RHXT YMPBHXLDF; TLD BHU EPLQEHY YLAP WT

USH UXMKKZQ KXLJ WLUS FZYHF.

—JMXBMXHU USMUQSHX

October 14

R'D GRFRUX WB PNK JOEBUY DE RUMBDO SLNS

HO DNE NGDBWS JO WNRY SB JO GRFRUX

NINKS. —O.O. MCDDRUXW

October 15

WRO RKHIEPH NDNZ ONNK R PZRSR AZLGLA LK

GWN PRHGLSN? EQ AETZON KEG! GWNH AESN

ETG RQGNZ PRZU, TB GE KE FEEP.

—B.F. JEPNWETON

....

October 16

BESHS WHS NWTL BEGTRX BEWB PS PIFAZ BEHIP

WPWL GO PS PSHS TIB WOHWGZ BEWB IBESHX

NGREB KGDC BESN FK.   —IXDWH PGAZS

....

October 17

WGO WGOLWOF HJ JY OBPNOJJNA CLJTHBLWHBQ

ROTLKJO HW'J JY LTTHPOBWLN. HW'J JY ZKTG

NHVO NHCO.   —LFWGKF ZHNNOF

....

October 18

KTRTIT PG T KCLRBOV SJCGD ZTPR DMHCOBG

TOD JCKEDV HXTVDOG TRI KCXI WOCRBG.

—HPDOOD BOLIDTL

October 19

CKGOSY JELM ZEEP NLMSFX OSNE K WEGOF OT

DOPF TFFOSY JELM EVFS NLMSFX OSNE

ZELODDES HLZFT.   —BECS DF HKMMF

October 20

C WODWBE DWILMR LN TML CILN JNOCLCGE, KHL

C DWE IMFMU OCTXL MINHTX LN PWVM LXM

LMWP.   —WUL KHGXDWOR

October 21

W'C U AGFSJOK FB VFMMNQFFS. BUZKUDN WD

ZFK JZZUKJGUM KF CY; WK'D CN GYUMWKN.

                    —OUGGWY BWDVYG

October 22

SB PWE AHP AW ZIRVEHI AXI BEAEHI, PWE DSFF

CIJIH HSVQ AXI YHIVICA.   —KRAXIHSCI LICIEJI

October 23

S WHC'P BSAY SP GZYC KYHKBY OIJP ERBB DY

"GYSVW." S'D CHP HC R LSVJP-RWOYEPSFY

XRJSJ GSPZ RCQXHWQ.

— "GYSVW" RB QRCAHFSE

October 24

ELD SHBO FHWE VOTFTEAR CHOVW AK ELD

DKZPAWL PTKZBTZD: "TRE HKD, WRDKD HKD."

— FHWW LTOE

October 25

FJFUO LYAWK AT MR MUBATB. BYF SUNZWFV AT

YNE BN UFVMAR MR MUBATB NRLF YF CUNET

QS.   — SMZWN SALMTTN

October 26

K NDDNTUSPER TUFKSM LAFU DUADEU AZ PCUKT

FAPCUT-KS-ENX AT PCUKT GALL AT LAFUPCKSY.

— CKEENTR JEKSPAS

October 27

H CHGE HO BLOMSB SLUX OP VPBOBLX L

JNUHGSUUDLG. JSHGZ JWLGE, BLOMSB QBNSW,

LGE HGQPDVSOSGO QPDSU GLONBLWWX OP DS.

—APMG QWSSUS

October 28

DT PRD ZODS BE RHTDSWF TY OF P

QWGLTGBPYRW; DT PRD ZODS BE RHTDSWF TLL

OF P XTRVBWYDPGE.   —KVHOP GTUWGDF

October 29

CHAG FVW NHVW GTGOWLSRCJW SH GWYTOSRHK.

SEWA'VW ZRNLG ZEWK RS OHNWG SH SEFS MRKY

HU GSTUU.   —ZRKHKF VAYWV

October 30

G QRCGS KLUSO'T WUITE ILTNYSTUKUAUEM UT

EY TQGDL QGSXT ZUEQ QUCTLAW.

—QLSIM ZUSDALI

··

October 31

Y ETSAJ VRDDTH KH VKCR EJYE THR JYD ET

VRYWH KD EJYE HTE RORWBLTZB PKDJRD BTS

PRVV.   — Z Y H   W Y E J R W

··

November 1

FO'M LHYHN JHHL GL FLABMONZ MHWNHO OTGO

MTIP JBMFLHMM FM HCGWODZ DFVH TFST

MWTIID, HCWHXO PFOT RILHZ.

                              — K H L L Z   R W W G N O T Z

··

November 2

B WHP'X FHU B EHF SCSG MLFX, JOX B EHF

JSEBMKSGSK LPWS ZLG XAGSS KHUF.

                              — K H P B S M   J L L P S

··

November 3

OTJNYBC D'Y QDUN B FBGI PKNGN D LBR QNBR

JC NQATP BXBDROI B JBRINQFDNLN BRY KBZN B

LTLUIBDQ.   — L K B G Q N O   A G T R O T R

84

November 4

BO DSH'E SZZ PO TOVLOF PODSCFO FLJOPLKQ

TSF EL FXE LH ETO DCVP SHK DZSY SF ETOQ WL

PQ.   —BXZZ VLWOVF

November 5

CHOFT KNLERF. EJXLYLZT HC'T L XJOLE XNJ'T

VLTCFQ JE CNF YQLX, LEY TNF KLE BQJMF HC LC

LEZ SLEG XHEYJX.   —QJZ QJRFQT

November 6

PHTUHA ZTBUFNH YH LFCI HPHTQS. FC'A LIHP F

NBP'C IRUH CIHY, LIHP F KHHG RC HRAH, CIRC

F QHC LBTTFHN.   —YFVH PFMIBGA

November 7

VABOW LT B GBP HK SDEELIS EAD BITGDO

"PDT" GLEAHRE BTCLIS B VNDBO JRDTELHI.

                                       —BNFDOE VBWRT

85

November 8

WXM TDYSN ALE BDYRHGM CYLAWHALSSI
LEIWXHER MFAMCW CMDCSM TXD KHEN WXMHY
DTE JOZHEMZZ. —KLYRLYMW KHWAXMSS

November 9

AF YIN BNNKNGY GNFGN, YIN GNCEVI PWE
NZYECYNEENGYEACT AFYNTTAMNFVN AG C
GNCEVI PWE WJEGNTQNG. —VCET GCMCF

November 10

MT MPWGN OL LGUCWROTZ DCLL WRMT M UMT,
QRODC MT MPWNCLL OL LGUCWROTZ UGNC WRMT
M QGUMT. —NOPRMNE JYNWGT

November 11

BFAB YTBCCH FY THCYDK GC GBD TCKD CN GBD
WVDKFTWQ DMODKFDQTD GBWQ WQSGBFQA DHYD
F TWQ GBFQR CN. —RPKG JCQQDAPG

HAV JUVVINQ NJ HAV BUVLL KNUYL OG LFXA D

KDZ HADH HAVUV OL GNH QFXA JUVVINQ JUNQ

OH. —WUDXV YVTTZ

JHWOAONG OG JLDEXJG AEL HFWK JDHTLGGOHF

THD QEONE FH JDLJXDXAOHF OG AEHCZEA

FLNLGGXDK. —DHULDA WHCOG GALMLFGHF

O DMVRPOVRD HMBIRT ON PHM PJOTID MN PJR

SWMGR OD FMXRTRI OB TRI FZTKRP.

—KTOBFR FJZTWRD

R LHWM SABXMVY. R KHRDW WLMT JMZHEYM

WLMG'VM ZLMHKMV WLHD TBCMAY HDC WLMG

CBD'W TBQM. —PMBVPRH B'FMMSSM

KPT JWGZ HO ZHLKHB W FNGK WD HGT FPH,

FPTG PT'D GHK TRNCWGWGU CT, WD PHCT

DKXZQWGU CTZWLWGT.   —UTHBUT D. JNXOCNG

L'D HNSNELNGF BNE YLALHY W TWJ LHSKEALKQ.

L'D WH WISNE WHJ L IWH'S VKUM TGS BKKU L'D

TNELHY QVKH L'D NH WF DOFKUB.

—ENIX VGJFNH

YIC SGOLCHO JMP BCY QHMK VDYCHSYPHC

ZCFCGZ PFMG YIC WPCOYDMGO JMP FMOC.

—KSHBSHCY SYLMMZ

PWNAN JO YQ LQUJPJVJHY JY JYMJH MHAJYB

NYQXBW PQ NFLUHJY PQ PWN GHOONO PWHP

VQDO VHY CN NHPNY.   —JYMJAH BHYMWJ

H QULJODDGLYHK GD DLZOLYO TCL PHY ML CGD

FODS TLUR TCOY CO MLODY'S JOOK KGRO GS.

—HKGDSHGU PLLRO

TWEXAM CVXLNP AWHO HLGGP. KB WRXOP FR

RXWRGX. KJ MWF'VX ZWWA, MWF TLO JKGG FR

BDWPX WRXOKOZP HKBD PWEXBDKOZ

RWPKBKQX.   —ZWGAKX DLHO

TUFRA L JWSUQURULF FAXAK YASUAXAT ZMLQ

MA TLGT, MA UT LSZLGT LTQWFUTMAO ZMAF

WQMAKT OW.   —RMLKSAT OA PLVSSA

TNGB V TLY BVBG, V DZLHGE QNG EGRWB JVBK

VB "IVBEGOGZZL," LBE VQ ZLCBINGE RG WB L

ZWBK LBE NLDDH ZVXG WX AGVBK L RWBYQGO.

—AWOVY JLOZWXX

November 24

CHQ KPLIHFEX: JACS TH SAF JPIHS SACS BCY

ACZZFY? SAFY ZIFZCIF SP CBBFZS TS. SAFY

ZIPBFFG SP TNZIPUF PY SAF JPIHS.

—GCEF BCIYFWTF

November 25

IL X JDCS CFTPD, X MIG FPLL IOOPEOXCE OC

SAIO ZPE LIG. X KHLO SIOVA SAIO OAPG TC.

—IETDPS VIDEPJXP

November 26

SLF OFDZ ELMR BHI QBGR TLG SLFGDRET,

PRQBFDR ZKBZ'D VKRH ZKR PRDZ QLORD LFZ.

—ZUHB ZFGHRG

November 27

CIL LFUWGAI GFACGFPCGOLWD HZEGTL HFD EHF

VIY IHA FY CHWLFC HFZ GA EYZLAC HQYRC GC.

—SHELA HULL

November 28

BR GKHE LF PLFLKUSHR KH LBSZLUSDLPN. DYSD

GYLAY ASU VN NCOMSLUNJ DK DYN LJLKD LF

UKD GKHDY BR ASHN. —GLMMLSB VMSEN

November 29

ERCM DRSNAY JNE COJHLUEHSG YUECD SG

QASERCD DS TC TSNAY VGST TRCG ERCM BS SNE

SP DEMAC. —BULLM DRUGYAHGB

November 30

VLDE XY EKZ TZODZE XY TWOOZTT AH JAYZ AT

EX ZLE GKLE BXW JAMZ LHQ JZE EKZ YXXQ

YACKE AE XWE AHTAQZ. —PLDM EGLAH

December 1

W YUPKAPS HR AUP NWRKE HN BQ BPAKLUQXWYX

POKBWRKAWHR. W EHHFPS WRAH AUP XHGE HN

AUP THQ XWAAWRD RPOA AH BP. —CHHSQ KEEPR

December 2

BREBUR GSH NE JR, "HEX WEF'N UEEV UMVR SF

SNIURNR, HEX UEEV UMVR S BRYGEF."

—JEFMKS GRURG

December 3

HMOXC F PYTFX OR F NMAAOHED UOLLOGWEN

NAFUM, ROXGM ON GYXRORNR VAOXGOVFEED YL

UMFEOXC PONB TMX.   —ZYRMVB GYXAFU

December 4

MO MN OYC JRKBOMGK GJ FMBC OG ZCCD

FMQORC EMOYMK QCPNGKPUAC UGRKTN.

—NPWRCA UROACQ

December 5

MN BMK MN G'D WYJWAKJAT, "VEYD" GN M VYKT

SEMS VMN GJIAJSAT SY DMCA AIAKXYJA NYHJT

PGCA M QHSPAK.   —WMPIGJ SKGPPGJ

December 6

F'D R VGUFVNGURM CFAFSWRUE. F TRW AGG

FWIS ING LHIHUG JHI XRE SLL IS ING AFZG.

—AIGCGW XUFPNI

December 7

PXTABGBKBHY AW DRE WBHPYREW PHN

WXTRVPEW. PY RHB YAKB A TPN PKJAYARHW,

JOY A TPN YTBK EBKRGBN JU P NRXYRE AH

JODDPVR.   —YRK ZPAYW

December 8

JE GHJ BOE OHF BCSFKASZ BRKO H

FSAQ-HZPVFKRJM WHCZ KHXAS WHJ SYSC XS

UVRKS KOS GHJ OS EJWS BHF. —PHGSF KOVCXSC

December 9

NG PHL TYES SH BEHT YUHLS Y CYE, PHL DYE

GNEF HLS YE YTGLW WHS UP WHHBNEA YS TZH

ZI CYMMNIF.   —BNMB FHLAWYR

December 10

YD Y DGGU ERBFYWPUUB PF YD JRG JVE VD LB

RGPT HGIG JPMGS VDD, Y MSVH JRPJ YF

EVGJIB.   —GLYUB TYWMYSFVS

December 11

QUO DHKAHQNGJ GS BHJRNJW KNOD GJKL NJ

BHRNJP OAOELQUNJP QUO MGJMOEJ GS HKK.

                     —HKOTHJWOE DGKCUOJNQDLJ

December 12

TRIMBTS BA DRKO MNDBWBHIBTS IMHT IR AOO

BPBRIA ANLLOOP BT OTIOKUKBAOA QO MHCO

EHBWOP BT.   —SNAIHCO EWHNVOKI

December 13

CNXOG CESS GOTOM JO LP PHKKOPPIHS LP XOG

JOKLHPO VWOR WLTO GN CETOP VN LBTEPO

VWOX.   —BEKA TLG BRAO

94

December 14

CWMG BL OCBRK. B QYGLL NUFN'L SUE BN
APWZGGKL OE NUG LGRLG WX NWYZU.

—TWPGE FTLNGPKFT

December 15

MN TRD AHL DO HCGST, JRGI SCLH, CPE OCT
TRDG LCBHF, TRD JMSS AHL CQHCE—MN TRD
FLGMIH RMS.　　　　　　—KHCP OCDS AHLLT

December 16

JOE OK FOCN PRYORA. OE KIXQFB ZN KNAYNB
OH KURFF, NFNWRHE SXAEOXHK RHB HXE
KSFRKINB RZXQE FOCN URAURFRBN.

—HXNF PXJRAB

December 17

ML LGARRMBDLL MB LRDDFU FTXLDW KP
MZBAHTBFD AH TRTSUP? M WAB'S QBAC TBW M
WAB'S FTHD.　　　　　—CMGGMTN LTVMHD

··

December 18

CRYFNAC WYE'R LGXA G BNWWDA YF GE AEW

GEPBYFA. RLAP KCKGDDP LGXA G ZAJNEENEJ

RLGR EAXAF CRYOC ZAJNEENEJ.

—CRAXAE CONADZAFJ

··

December 19

BUPNNAHJAY WPFA TRD MCYBRLAG SUCHJY

PVRDS TRDGYANZ SUPS TRD HALAG GAPNNT

FHAX. —BCBANT STYRH

··

December 20

Z GKDA K NZLBIA BWZMSZBIA TRW HGA

SRMPVSH RT IZTA—MADAW HR WANZNH KM

KPAFVKHA HALBHKHZRM. —LKY IAWMAW

··

December 21

TVH MOE UHE OE VLLBMD KBSAVHS O JVZZ,

JHS TVH MOE'S UHE OE VLLBMD KBSAVHS

ZDMUDSOUBDZ. —POED LVEGO

December 22

DAT QHR RNE NWTLUNPT GARFTGG CG DN

VTUNPT GN QLHBBTM EB CF GNPTDACFI DAHD

RNE ONLITD DN VT HOLHCM.

—SHMR VCLM ZNAFGNF

December 23

OVCCLCY LP PEMG JI PEMG. LN IWV YW PEMG JI

PEMG, IWV'DD RDARIP LSGOWTM. L DLZM EBRE

RJWVE OVCCLCY.   —JLDD OWUYMOP

December 24

DOB DANB UBLGVGY MS ABZVYVMG VP GMD

PVUKZE UMALZVDE HND UMALZVDE DMNTOBX HE

BUMDVMG.   —ULDDOBR LAGMZX

December 25

UQ GO GWYRN TGD G HXDDGAX, TX DTRJFB

WGFF KXDYXNO JOURO. GO GWYRN'D SRE UD YR

GWY, ORYTUOA HRNX.   —TJHLTNXM ERAGNY

December 26

NQ DPA HBKE EP MWBX BTPAE UPRW BKX

CBMMNBJW, DPA'RW JPE EP TAD EHP YWGBMBEW

TPPZY. —BUBK ZNKJ

December 27

BLO GOWPBAXKCLAM FOBHOOK BLO ZPDO-JM

ZPK PKV BLO YAWZ PQBXG AC BLPB XY

PQQXZMWAQOC AK QGAZO. —ZPGWOKO VAOBGAQL

December 28

G THWIM EVAVJ JVPM P CHHD GN GS TVJV

QHFFGCIV NHJ ZV SH SPID KPIN PE KHWJ TGSK

SKV ZPE TKH TJHSV GS. —THHMJHT TGIFHE

December 29

TWG NOC'D KZ KVORZ FA TWG'RZ WCXT MOE

QWCEZVAGX DMFCPY MOBBZC DW TWG.

—JOVT DTXZV JWWVZ

December 30

THEEHY REHLTOX GHE PHLEDXOG, CG RKFR'D
PHLE JFRLEX, TLR WHJ'R OXJW CR RH PHLE
JXCZKTHED.   —ELWPFEW VCMOCJZ

December 31

WOSES YN KHWOYKZ LHES CYBBYPRDW BHE Q
WERDX PESQWYJS FQYKWSE WOQK WH FQYKW Q
EHNS.   —OSKEY LQWYNNS

FIRST HINTS

Occupation and Year of Birth

Jan. 1: senator (1909)
Feb. 1: movie performer (1901)
Mar. 1: movie director (1954)
Apr. 1: movie performer (1883)
May 1: movie performer (1916)
Jun. 1: movie performer (1926)
Jul. 1: movie performer (1931)
Aug. 1: singer (1942)
Sep. 1: comedian (1939)
Oct. 1: movie performer (1920)
Nov. 1: television performer (1972)
Dec. 1: movie performer/director (1935)

Jan. 2: author (1920)
Feb. 2: author (1905)
Mar. 2: author (1931)
Apr. 2: comedian (1955)
May 2: physician/author (1903)
Jun. 2: author (1840)
Jul. 2: political figure (1931)
Aug. 2: author (1924)
Sep. 2: movie performer (1964)
Oct. 2: comedian (1890)
Nov. 2: pioneer (1734)
Dec. 2: tennis player (1973)

Jan. 3: comic pianist (1909)
Feb. 3: author (1874)
Mar. 3: movie performer (1911)
Apr. 3: movie performer (1924)
May 3: world leader (1898)
Jun. 3: movie performer (1911)
Jul. 3: newspaper columnist (1947)
Aug. 3: domestic entrepreneur (1941)
Sep. 3: television panelist (1915)
Oct. 3: author (1925)
Nov. 3: movie performer (1922)
Dec. 3: author (1857)

Jan. 4: scientist (1643)
Feb. 4: vice president (1947)
Mar. 4: football coach (1888)
Apr. 4: poet (1928)
May 4: magazine columnist (1941)
Jun. 4: movie performer (1911)
Jul. 4: newspaper columnist (1918)
Aug. 4: poet (1792)
Sep. 4: broadcast journalist (1918)
Oct. 4: movie performer (1922)
Nov. 4: comedian (1879)
Dec. 4: author (1835)

Jan. 5: vice president (1928)
Feb. 5: presidential candidate (1900)
Mar. 5: movie performer (1908)
Apr. 5: movie performer (1900)
May 5: chef (1903)
Jun. 5: broadcast journalist (1934)
Jul. 5: poet/movie director (1889)
Aug. 5: movie director (1906)
Sep. 5: television performer (1929)
Oct. 5: business executive (1902)
Nov. 5: television performer (1912)
Dec. 5: author (1935)

Jan. 6: poet (1878)
Feb. 6: president (1911)
Mar. 6: author (1885)
Apr. 6: singer (1937)
May 6: movie performer/director (1915)
Jun. 6: author (1875)
Jul. 6: first lady (1921)
Aug. 6: television performer (1911)
Sep. 6: presidential father (1888)
Oct. 6: movie performer (1909)
Nov. 6: movie director (1931)
Dec. 6: comedian (1955)

Jan. 7: singer (1948)
Feb. 7: author (1812)
Mar. 7: weather forecaster (1934)
Apr. 7: newspaper columnist (1897)
May 7: football player (1933)
Jun. 7: singer (1958)
Jul. 7: baseball player (1906)
Aug. 7: radio personality/author (1942)
Sep. 7: singer (1951)
Oct. 7: scientist (1885)
Nov. 7: author/philosopher (1913)
Dec. 7: singer (1949)

Jan. 8: broadcast journalist (1933)
Feb. 8: movie performer (1925)
Mar. 8: movie performer (1943)
Apr. 8: comedian (1926)
May 8: president (1884)
Jun. 8: comedian (1937)
Jul. 8: business executive (1839)
Aug. 8: movie performer (1937)
Sep. 8: television performer (1922)
Oct. 8: children's author (1943)
Nov. 8: author (1900)
Dec. 8: author (1894)

Jan. 9: president (1913)
Feb. 9: author (1944)
Mar. 9: author (1918)
Apr. 9: comic pianist (1928)
May 9: singer (1949)
Jun. 9: comedian (1934)
Jul. 9: author (1901)
Aug. 9: television performer (1968)
Sep. 9: author (1828)
Oct. 9: singer (1940)
Nov. 9: astronomer (1934)
Dec. 9: movie performer (1916)

Jan. 10: boxer (1949)
Feb. 10: opera singer (1927)
Mar. 10: movie performer (1958)
Apr. 10: author/politician (1903)

May 10: singer (1960)
Jun. 10: royal consort (1921)
Jul. 10: author (1871)
Aug. 10: president (1874)
Sep. 10: golfer (1929)
Oct. 10: tennis player (1956)
Nov. 10: movie performer (1925)
Dec. 10: poet (1830)

Jan. 11: philosopher (1842)
Feb. 11: movie performer (1936)
Mar. 11: author (1952)
Apr. 11: politician (1893)
May 11: songwriter (1888)
Jun. 11: football coach (1913)
Jul. 11: boxer (1953)
Aug. 11: magazine columnist (1946)
Sep. 11: football coach (1913)
Oct. 11: first lady (1884)
Nov. 11: author (1922)
Dec. 11: author (1918)

Jan. 12: comedian (1906)
Feb. 12: president (1809)
Mar. 12: singer (1948)
Apr. 12: singer (1957)
May 12: comedian (1937)
Jun. 12: president (1924)
Jul. 12: television performer (1937)
Aug. 12: movie producer (1881)
Sep. 12: singer (1888)
Oct. 12: opera singer (1935)
Nov. 12: movie performer (1929)
Dec. 12: author (1821)

Jan. 13: television performer (1961)
Feb. 13: movie performer (1934)
Mar. 13: religious leader (1911)
Apr. 13: president (1743)
May 13: singer (1950)
Jun. 13: television performer (1953)
Jul. 13: movie performer (1942)
Aug. 13: movie performer (1895)
Sep. 13: newspaper columnist (1938)

Oct. 13: world leader (1925)
Nov. 13: author (1850)
Dec. 13: television performer (1925)

Jan. 14: television commentator (1919)
Feb. 14: television performer (1894)
Mar. 14: scientist (1879)
Apr. 14: baseball player (1941)
May 14: singer (1952)
Jun. 14: business executive (1946)
Jul. 14: movie director (1918)
Aug. 14: comedian (1945)
Sep. 14: movie performer (1947)
Oct. 14: poet (1894)
Nov. 14: world leader (1948)
Dec. 14: comedian (1914)

Jan. 15: business executive (1906)
Feb. 15: stage performer (1882)
Mar. 15: football player (1926)
Apr. 15: author (1843)
May 15: movie performer (1951)
Jun. 15: governor (1932)
Jul. 15: comic poet (1906)
Aug. 15: chef (1912)
Sep. 15: author (1890)
Oct. 15: author (1881)
Nov. 15: painter (1887)
Dec. 15: business executive (1892)

Jan. 16: singer (1909)
Feb. 16: ventriloquist (1903)
Mar. 16: movie performer (1926)
Apr. 16: movie performer/director (1889)
May 16: movie performer (1905)
Jun. 16: author (1937)
Jul. 16: movie performer/dancer (1911)
Aug. 16: singer (1958)
Sep. 16: singer (1925)
Oct. 16: playwright (1854)
Nov. 16: playwright (1889)
Dec. 16: playwright (1899)

Jan. 17: writer/inventor/politician (1706)
Feb. 17: basketball player (1963)
Mar. 17: movie performer (1899)
Apr. 17: world leader (1894)
May 17: movie performer (1955)
Jun. 17: composer (1882)
Jul. 17: comedian (1917)
Aug. 17: movie performer (1892)
Sep. 17: author (1935)
Oct. 17: playwright (1915)
Nov. 17: movie performer (1925)
Dec. 17: newspaper columnist (1929)

Jan. 18: movie performer (1904)
Feb. 18: author (1931)
Mar. 18: author (1932)
Apr. 18: lawyer (1857)
May 18: philosopher/mathematician (1872)
Jun. 18: movie critic (1942)
Jul. 18: author (1811)
Aug. 18: movie performer (1922)
Sep. 18: author (1709)
Oct. 18: world leader (1919)
Nov. 18: author (1939)
Dec. 18: movie director (1947)

Jan. 19: author (1809)
Feb. 19: movie performer (1924)
Mar. 19: author (1933)
Apr. 19: movie performer (1935)
May 19: world leader (1879)
Jun. 19: bandleader (1902)
Jul. 19: painter (1834)
Aug. 19: comic poet (1902)
Sep. 19: singer (1964)
Oct. 19: author (1931)
Nov. 19: world leader (1917)
Dec. 19: movie performer (1933)

Jan. 20: comedian (1896)
Feb. 20: movie director (1925)
Mar. 20: playwright (1828)

Apr. 20: movie performer (1949)
May 20: singer/movie performer (1946)
Jun. 20: movie performer (1909)
Jul. 20: movie performer (1938)
Aug. 20: boxing promoter (1931)
Sep. 20: movie performer (1934)
Oct. 20: newspaper columnist (1925)
Nov. 20: television host (1908)
Dec. 20: journalist/author (1902)

Jan. 21: golfer (1940)
Feb. 21: newspaper columnist (1927)
Mar. 21: television host (1962)
Apr. 21: world leader (1926)
May 21: business executive (1898)
Jun. 21: philosopher/author (1905)
Jul. 21: author (1899)
Aug. 21: singer (1938)
Sep. 21: author (1947)
Oct. 21: movie performer/author (1956)
Nov. 21: movie performer (1945)
Dec. 21: movie performer/fitness expert (1937)

Jan. 22: poet (1788)
Feb. 22: movie performer (1975)
Mar. 22: musical composer (1930)
Apr. 22: movie performer (1937)
May 22: author (1859)
Jun. 22: movie director (1906)
Jul. 22: presidential candidate (1923)
Aug. 22: author (1920)
Sep. 22: baseball manager (1927)
Oct. 22: movie performer (1943)
Nov. 22: world leader (1890)
Dec. 22: first lady (1912)

Jan. 23: movie performer (1928)
Feb. 23: diarist (1633)
Mar. 23: movie performer (1908)

Apr. 23: singer (1936)
May 23: television performer/author (1933)
Jun. 23: television performer (1946)
Jul. 23: author (1888)
Aug. 23: comic pianist (1932)
Sep. 23: singer (1949)
Oct. 23: comic singer (1959)
Nov. 23: movie performer (1887)
Dec. 23: marathoner (1947)

Jan. 24: author (1862)
Feb. 24: business executive (1955)
Mar. 24: movie performer (1930)
Apr. 24: movie performer (1934)
May 24: movie performer (1946)
Jun. 24: author (1842)
Jul. 24: aviator (1898)
Aug. 24: movie performer (1965)
Sep. 24: author (1896)
Oct. 24: playwright (1904)
Nov. 24: self-help author (1888)
Dec. 24: poet (1822)

Jan. 25: author (1874)
Feb. 25: author (1917)
Mar. 25: author (1925)
Apr. 25: movie performer (1940)
May 25: essayist (1803)
Jun. 25: author (1903)
Jul. 25: presidential brother (1956)
Aug. 25: singer (1955)
Sep. 25: television journalist (1931)
Oct. 25: painter (1881)
Nov. 25: business executive (1835)
Dec. 25: movie performer (1899)

Jan. 26: movie performer (1925)
Feb. 26: television performer (1920)
Mar. 26: poet (1874)
Apr. 26: television performer (1936)
May 26: movie performer (1907)
Jun. 26: author (1892)
Jul. 26: comedian (1906)

Aug. 26: playwright (1904)
Sep. 26: fitness expert (1914)
Oct. 26: first lady (1947)
Nov. 26: singer (1939)
Dec. 26: comedian (1927)

Jan. 27: author (1832)
Feb. 27: author (1902)
Mar. 27: movie director (1963)
Apr. 27: president (1822)
May 27: politician (1923)
Jun. 27: presidential candidate
(1930)
Jul. 27: baseball manager (1906)
Aug. 27: movie producer (1882)
Sep. 27: author (1917)
Oct. 27: comedian (1939)
Nov. 27: author (1909)
Dec. 27: movie performer (1901)

Jan. 28: dancer (1948)
Feb. 28: poet (1909)
Mar. 28: singer (1955)
Apr. 28: television host (1950)
May 28: author (1908)
Jun. 28: movie performer/director
(1926)
Jul. 28: singer (1901)
Aug. 28: author (1749)
Sep. 28: cartoonist (1909)
Oct. 28: movie performer (1967)
Nov. 28: poet (1757)
Dec. 28: president (1856)

Jan. 29: comedian (1880)
Feb. 29: composer (1792)
Mar. 29: singer (1918)
Apr. 29: television performer (1955)
May 29: president (1917)
Jun. 29: comedian (1947)
Jul. 29: lawyer (1907)
Aug. 29: movie performer (1915)
Sep. 29: world leader (1943)
Oct. 29: movie performer (1971)
Nov. 29: television performer (1949)
Dec. 29: television performer (1937)

Jan. 30: president (1882)
Mar. 30: movie performer (1937)
Apr. 30: singer (1933)
May 30: stage performer/author
(1901)
Jun. 30: boxer (1966)
Jul. 30: baseball manager (1890)
Aug. 30: baseball player (1918)
Sep. 30: author (1924)
Oct. 30: television performer (1945)
Nov. 30: author (1835)
Dec. 30: poet (1865)

Jan. 31: movie performer (1903)
Mar. 31: vice president (1948)
May 31: self-help author (1898)
Jul. 31: politician/author (1943)
Aug. 31: television host (1903)
Oct. 31: television journalist (1931)
Dec. 31: painter (1869)

SECOND HINTS

A Letter or More

Jan. 1: E represents N.
Feb. 1: F represents T.
Mar. 1: J represents N.
Apr. 1: T represents P.
May 1: E represents Y.
Jun. 1: TLR represents YOU.
Jul. 1: C represents W.
Aug. 1: N represents U.
Sep. 1: H represents L.
Oct. 1: V represents M.
Nov. 1: W represents C.
Dec. 1: WRD represents ING.

Jan. 2: R represents I.
Feb. 2: TO appears twice.
Mar. 2: V represents W.
Apr. 2: F represents L.
May 2: C represents H.
Jun. 2: L represents O.
Jul. 2: ER represents TH.
Aug. 2: D represents V.
Sep. 2: B represents P.
Oct. 2: E represents N.
Nov. 2: S represents E.
Dec. 2: V represents K.

Jan. 3: IHD represents BUT.
Feb. 3: K represents S.
Mar. 3: C represents D.
Apr. 3: N represents G.
May 3: JO represents TH.
Jun. 3: The first word is IF.
Jul. 3: S represents E.
Aug. 3: H represents A.
Sep. 3: NX represents TV.
Oct. 3: RWB represents ONE.
Nov. 3: BRY represents AND.
Dec. 3: OXC represents ING.

Jan. 4: B represents T.
Feb. 4: H represents Y.
Mar. 4: FTTK represents GOOD.

Apr. 4: M represents T.
May 4: R represents E.
Jun. 4: H represents R.
Jul. 4: IKR represents THE.
Aug. 4: R represents Y.
Sep. 4: V represents T.
Oct. 4: LE represents ED.
Nov. 4: PO represents BE.
Dec. 4: ZCCD represents KEEP.

Jan. 5: L represents U.
Feb. 5: M represents D.
Mar. 5: G represents R.
Apr. 5: C represents W.
May 5: E represents V.
Jun. 5: G represents E.
Jul. 5: E represents R.
Aug. 5: S represents T.
Sep. 5: I represents H.
Oct. 5: J represents P.
Nov. 5: SLEG represents
         BANK.
Dec. 5: I represents V.

Jan. 6: R represents H.
Feb. 6: QHLL represents NESS.
Mar. 6: T represents W.
Apr. 6: D represents M.
May 6: Z represents Y.
Jun. 6: G represents S.
Jul. 6: B represents N.
Aug. 6: Two words end with LY.
Sep. 6: C represents U.
Oct. 6: F represents W.
Nov. 6: Y represents M.
Dec. 6: I represents T.

Jan. 7: M represents L.
Feb. 7: A represents K.
Mar. 7: C represents F.
Apr. 7: The longest word ends
         with ALLY.
May 7: R represents D.

Jun. 7: H represents O.
Jul. 7: M represents S.
Aug. 7: P represents G.
Sep. 7: T represents Y.
Oct. 7: R represents H.
Nov. 7: E represents T.
Dec. 7: BN represents ED.

Jan. 8: O represents N.
Feb. 8: The first word is IF.
Mar. 8: E represents O.
Apr. 8: DIL and LWBC are
  initials of famous schools.
May 8: Z represents Y.
Jun. 8: TZZ represents ALL.
Jul. 8: F represents G.
Aug. 8: OZ represents IN.
Sep. 8: C represents T.
Oct. 8: R represents E.
Nov. 8: X represents H.
Dec. 8: F represents S.

Jan. 9: C represents I.
Feb. 9: S represents F.
Mar. 9: N represents H.
Apr. 9: D represents H.
May 9: E represents W.
Jun. 9: D represents T.
Jul. 9: N represents F.
Aug. 9: P represents T.
Sep. 9: N represents O.
Oct. 9: T represents W.
Nov. 9: G represents S.
Dec. 9: P represents Y.

Jan. 10: Y represents G.
Feb. 10: TNA represents YOU.
Mar. 10: P represents T.
Apr. 10: H represents I.
May 10: H represents W.
Jun. 10: B represents W.
Jul. 10: H represents N.
Aug. 10: L represents H.
Sep. 10: D represents T.
Oct. 10: F represents M.

Nov. 10: P represents C.
Dec. 10: D represents F.

Jan. 11: H represents T.
Feb. 11: WT represents ON.
Mar. 11: H represents D.
Apr. 11: V represents T.
May 11: A represents H.
Jun. 11: S represents L.
Jul. 11: P represents L.
Aug. 11: Y represents G.
Sep. 11: E represents S.
Oct. 11: R represents O.
Nov. 11: D represents E.
Dec. 11: P represents G.

Jan. 12: B represents Y.
Feb. 12: N represents A.
Mar. 12: G represents T.
Apr. 12: P represents C.
May 12: Three words end with
  ING.
Jun. 12: B represents G.
Jul. 12: JHS represents BUT.
Aug. 12: E represents K.
Sep. 12: W represents M.
Oct. 12: W represents M.
Nov. 12: A represents H.
Dec. 12: OP represents ED.

Jan. 13: Three words end with
  ING.
Feb. 13: B represents G.
Mar. 13: T represents N.
Apr. 13: Q represents W.
May 13: D represents P.
Jun. 13: T represents E.
Jul. 13: G represents H.
Aug. 13: Q represents Z.
Sep. 13: The longest word ends
  with IVE.
Oct. 13: THE appears three times.
Nov. 13: AEL represents THE.
Dec. 13: VWOR and VWOX are
  pronouns.

Jan. 14: O represents L.
Feb. 14: AND appears three times.
Mar. 14: THE and AND both appear twice.
Apr. 14: The hyphenated word is a number.
May 14: A represents V.
Jun. 14: EP represents TH.
Jul. 14: K represents V.
Aug. 14: N represents O.
Sep. 14: K represents N.
Oct. 14: RUX represents ING.
Nov. 14: H represents W.
Dec. 14: L represents S.

Jan. 15: U represents N.
Feb. 15: The contraction ends N'T.
Mar. 15: L represents V.
Apr. 15: F represents N.
May 15: EF represents ON.
Jun. 15: B represents C.
Jul. 15: B represents U.
Aug. 15: GI represents IT.
Sep. 15: PB represents HE.
Oct. 15: O represents S.
Nov. 15: WL represents TH.
Dec. 15: JMSS represents WILL.

Jan. 16: M represents L.
Feb. 16: V represents N.
Mar. 16: The longest word begins with INT.
Apr. 16: K represents R.
May 16: O represents C.
Jun. 16: S represents Y.
Jul. 16: E represents H.
Aug. 16: ATK represents ING.
Sep. 16: O represents M.
Oct. 16: PS represents WE.
Nov. 16: F represents W.
Dec. 16: HXE represents NOT.

Jan. 17: The first word is IF.
Feb. 17: N represents T.
Mar. 17: P'OW represents I'VE.

Apr. 17: L represents E.
May 17: E represents D.
Jun. 17: Y represents G.
Jul. 17: AS represents TO.
Aug. 17: L represents V.
Sep. 17: B represents E.
Oct. 17: T represents C.
Nov. 17: B represents F.
Dec. 17: F represents C.

Jan. 18: K represents T.
Feb. 18: PS represents IT.
Mar. 18: C represents H.
Apr. 18: S represents T.
May 18: G represents E.
Jun. 18: F represents E.
Jul. 18: J represents W.
Aug. 18: P represents L.
Sep. 18: BS represents ED.
Oct. 18: O represents R.
Nov. 18: YOU appears twice.
Dec. 18: E represents N.

Jan. 19: G represents H.
Feb. 19: TD represents IS.
Mar. 19: OS represents IN.
Apr. 19: X represents D.
May 19: V represents N.
Jun. 19: CL represents HE.
Jul. 19: C represents D.
Aug. 19: KWD represents YOU.
Sep. 19: I represents N.
Oct. 19: OSY represents ING.
Nov. 19: P represents T.
Dec. 19: D represents U.

Jan. 20: OS represents ER.
Feb. 20: G represents R.
Mar. 20: EH represents TO.
Apr. 20: G represents V.
May 20: T represents Y.
Jun. 20: D represents Y.
Jul. 20: C represents W.
Aug. 20: P represents T.
Sep. 20: B represents P.

Oct. 20: W represents A.
Nov. 20: R represents K.
Dec. 20: D represents V.

Jan. 21: TVX represents YOU.
Feb. 21: WHEN appears twice.
Mar. 21: S represents D.
Apr. 21: F represents T.
May 21: AOXOP and
           JHRFEOOP are numbers.
Jun. 21: F represents R.
Jul. 21: H represents F.
Aug. 21: B represents K.
Sep. 21: PGAR represents
           TION.
Oct. 21: N represents Y.
Nov. 21: M represents Y.
Dec. 21: The first word is YOU.

Jan. 22: WT represents NO.
Feb. 22: V represents T.
Mar. 22: J represents P.
Apr. 22: T represents E.
May 22: E represents N.
Jun. 22: T represents P.
Jul. 22: L represents O.
Aug. 22: Z represents O.
Sep. 22: THW represents AND.
Oct. 22: E represents U.
Nov. 22: The middle part of the
           name is DE.
Dec. 22: G represents S.

Jan. 23: Y represents N.
Feb. 23: G represents P.
Mar. 23: Z represents T.
Apr. 23: P represents V.
May 23: J represents I.
Jun. 23: L represents C.
Jul. 23: DBE represents CAN.
Aug. 23: S represents G.
Sep. 23: B represents E.
Oct. 23: C represents N.
Nov. 23: B represents N.
Dec. 23: Y represents G.

Jan. 24: D represents P.
Feb. 24: D represents N.
Mar. 24: U represents E.
Apr. 24: L represents O.
May 24: E represents V.
Jun. 24: H represents R.
Jul. 24: E represents T.
Aug. 24: B represents O.
Sep. 24: H represents O.
Oct. 24: AR represents IC.
Nov. 24: B represents C.
Dec. 24: G represents N.

Jan. 25: QTE represents FOR.
Feb. 25: V represents N.
Mar. 25: U represents E.
Apr. 25: SHY represents NOT.
May 25: IT represents AN.
Jun. 25: N represents G.
Jul. 25: J represents D.
Aug. 25: Three words end with
           ING.
Sep. 25: L represents A.
Oct. 25: T represents S.
Nov. 25: KHLO represents JUST.
Dec. 25: W represents C.

Jan. 26: LEO represents ION.
Feb. 26: TYD represents WHO.
Mar. 26: Two words end with LY.
Apr. 26: ORY represents ING.
May 26: O represents H.
Jun. 26: Y represents D.
Jul. 26: Two words are months.
Aug. 26: PL represents IS.
Sep. 26: G represents C.
Oct. 26: D represents P.
Nov. 26: H represents N.
Dec. 26: T represents B.

Jan. 27: J represents W.
Feb. 27: The quotation's last word
           ends with NESS.
Mar. 27: X represents G.
Apr. 27: O represents S.

May 27: O represents H.
Jun. 27: THE appears six times.
Jul. 27: O represents M.
Aug. 27: W represents D.
Sep. 27: Two words end with TION.
Oct. 27: OP represents TO.
Nov. 27: I represents H.
Dec. 27: O represents E.

Jan. 28: T represents N.
Feb. 28: H represents G.
Mar. 28: T represents S.
Apr. 28: W represents T.
May 28: T represents O.
Jun. 28: H represents N.
Jul. 28: M represents N.
Aug. 28: H represents N.
Sep. 28: The second word is ART.
Oct. 28: TLL represents OFF.
Nov. 28: L represents I.
Dec. 28: V represents E.

Jan. 29: C represents W.
Feb. 29: L represents N.
Mar. 29: GDXN represents JUST.
Apr. 29: YHCA represents SAME.

May 29: Two words end with ING.
Jun. 29: B represents W.
Jul. 29: F represents K.
Aug. 29: C represents W.
Sep. 29: A represents D.
Oct. 29: The contraction ends 'RE.
Nov. 29: SNE represents OUT.
Dec. 29: T represents Y.

Jan. 30: THE appears four times.
Mar. 30: Y represents D.
Apr. 30: K represents W.
May 30: L represents N.
Jun. 30: L represents T.
Jul. 30: A represents Y.
Aug. 30: G represents W.
Sep. 30: A represents N.
Oct. 30: E represents T.
Nov. 30: OF appears twice.
Dec. 30: G represents F.

Jan. 31: C represents G.
Mar. 31: THE appears four times.
May 31: Y represents E.
Jul. 31: L represents N.
Aug. 31: Q represents H.
Oct. 31: E represents T.
Dec. 31: B represents F.

ANSWERS

January 1
Running for the presidency is something like trying to stand up in a hammock.
—Barry Goldwater (1/1/1909)

January 2
Life is pleasant. Death is peaceful. It's the transition that's troublesome.
—Isaac Asimov (1/2/1920)

January 3
In my youth I wanted to be a great pantomimist, but I found I had nothing to say.
—Victor Borge (1/3/1909)

January 4
If I have been able to see farther than others, it was because I stood on the shoulders of giants.
—Isaac Newton (1/4/1643)

January 5
If you are sure you understand everything that is going on, you are hopelessly confused.
—Walter Mondale (1/5/1928)

January 6
Slang is language which takes off its coat, spits on its hands, and goes to work. —Carl Sandburg (1/6/1878)

January 7
We all long for love. Whether we know it or not, everything else we do is just killing time.
—Kenny Loggins (1/7/1948)

January 8
Even in one's own area of expertise, the longer you study and specialize, the more you know about less and less. —Charles Osgood (1/8/1933)

January 9
If an individual wants to be a leader and isn't controversial, that means he never stood for anything.
—Richard M. Nixon (1/9/1913)

January 10
I want to keep fighting because it is the only thing that keeps me out of the hamburger joints.
—George Foreman (1/10/1949)

January 11
There is only one thing a philosopher can be relied on to do, and that is to contradict other philosophers.
—William James (1/11/1842)

January 12
If you're going to do something tonight you'll be sorry for tomorrow morning, sleep late.
—Henny Youngman (1/12/1906)

January 13
We are not solving the economy and we are not curing cancer. We are just trying to make a good joke.
—Julia Louis-Dreyfus (1/13/1961)

January 14
We're all proud of making little mistakes. It gives us the feeling we don't make any big ones.
—Andy Rooney (1/14/1919)

January 15

If women didn't exist, all the money in the world would have no meaning.
—Aristotle Onassis (1/15/1906)

January 16

Always give them the old fire, even when you feel like a squashed cake of ice.   —Ethel Merman (1/16/1909)

January 17

If you would like to know the value of money, go and try to borrow some.
—Benjamin Franklin (1/17/1706)

January 18

I pretended to be somebody I wanted to be until I finally became that person—or he became me.
—Cary Grant (1/18/1904)

January 19

Of puns it has been said that they who most dislike them are least able to utter them.
—Edgar Allan Poe (1/19/1809)

January 20

I should have been a country-western singer. After all, I'm older than most western countries.
—George Burns (1/20/1896)

January 21

The older you get, the stronger the wind gets—and it's always in your face.   —Jack Nicklaus (1/21/1940)

January 22

One of the pleasures of reading old letters is the knowledge that they need no answer.
—George Gordon Byron (1/22/1788)

January 23

There are never ten ways to do something, only one. That is a question of morality.
—Jeanne Moreau (1/23/1928)

January 24

If only we'd stop trying to be happy, we'd have a pretty good time.
—Edith Wharton (1/24/1862)

January 25

There are three rules for writing a novel. Unfortunately, no one knows what they are.
—W. Somerset Maugham (1/25/1874)

January 26

I wasn't driven to acting by an inner compulsion. I was running away from the sporting goods business.
—Paul Newman (1/26/1925)

January 27

If you limit your actions in life to things that nobody can possibly find fault with, you will not do much.
—Lewis Carroll (1/27/1832)

January 28

I do not try to dance better than anyone else. I only try to dance better than myself.
—Mikhail Baryshnikov (1/28/1948)

January 29

Women are like elephants to me; they're nice to look at but I wouldn't want to own one.
—W.C. Fields (1/29/1880)

January 30

I think we consider too much the good luck of the early bird and not enough the bad luck of the early worm.
—Franklin D. Roosevelt (1/30/1882)

January 31

It's the good girls who keep the diaries; the bad girls never have the time.
—Tallulah Bankhead (1/31/1903)

February 1

The only reason they come to see me is that I know that life is great—and they know I know it.
—Clark Gable (2/1/1901)

February 2

The hardest thing to explain is the glaringly evident which everybody had decided not to see.
—Ayn Rand (2/2/1905)

February 3

Everybody gets so much information all day long that they lose their common sense.
—Gertrude Stein (2/3/1874)

February 4

How you exit is important—especially if you're thinking of coming back.
—Dan Quayle (2/4/1947)

February 5

An editor is one who separates the wheat from the chaff and prints the chaff. —Adlai Stevenson (2/5/1900)

February 6

Money can't buy happiness but it will certainly get you a better class of memories.
—Ronald Reagan (2/6/1911)

February 7

Take nothing on its looks; take everything on evidence. There's no better rule.
—Charles Dickens (2/7/1812)

February 8

If you think it's hard to meet new people, try picking up the wrong golf ball. —Jack Lemmon (2/8/1925)

February 9

Life is better than death, I believe, if only because it is less boring and because it has fresh peaches in it.
—Alice Walker (2/9/1944)

February 10

The ultimate of being successful is the luxury of giving yourself the time to do what you want to do.
—Leontyne Price (2/10/1927)

February 11

My movies are the kind they show in prisons and on airplanes because nobody can leave.
—Burt Reynolds (2/11/1936)

February 12

When you have got an elephant by the hind legs and he is trying to run away, it is best to let him run.
—Abraham Lincoln (2/12/1809)

February 13

The good thing about the movies is that you can eat and meditate at the same time.

—George Segal (2/13/1934)

February 14

Give me my golf clubs, fresh air, and a beautiful partner, and you can keep my golf clubs and the fresh air.

—Jack Benny (2/14/1894)

February 15

One of my chief regrets during my years in the theater is that I couldn't sit in the audience and watch me.

—John Barrymore (2/15/1882)

February 16

Hard work never killed anybody, but why take a chance on being the first?

—Edgar Bergen (2/16/1903)

February 17

I'm not out there sweating for three hours every day just to find out what it feels like to sweat.

—Michael Jordan (2/17/1963)

February 18

If there is a book you really want to read but it hasn't been written yet, then you must write it.

—Toni Morrison (2/18/1931)

February 19

Love is generally valued at its highest during two periods in life: the days of courting and the days in court.

—Lee Marvin (2/19/1924)

February 20

Nobody has ever made a good movie. Someday someone will make half a good one.

—Robert Altman (2/20/1925)

February 21

When my kids become wild and unruly, I use a nice, safe playpen. When they're finished, I climb out.

—Erma Bombeck (2/21/1927)

February 22

I always had to touch the stove to see how hot it was. I was never one of those who could just hear about it.

—Drew Barrymore (2/22/1975)

February 23

Strange to say what delight we married people have to see these poor fools decoyed into our condition.

—Samuel Pepys (2/23/1633)

February 24

Lincoln did not have a Web site at the log cabin where his parents home-schooled him, and he turned out pretty interesting.

—Steve Jobs (2/24/55)

February 25

Laugh and the world laughs with you; snore and you sleep alone.

—Anthony Burgess (2/25/1917)

February 26

Every time I find a girl who can cook like my mother, she looks like my father.   —Tony Randall (2/26/1920)

February 27
The profession of book writing
makes horse racing seem like a solid,
stable business.
— John Steinbeck (2/27/1902)

February 28
Great poetry is always written by
somebody straining to go beyond
what he can do.
— Stephen Spender (2/28/1909)

February 29
One cannot judge "Lohengrin" from
a first hearing, and I certainly do not
intend to hear it a second time.
— Gioacchino Rossini (2/29/1792)

March 1
There's nothing wrong with
teenagers that reasoning with them
won't aggravate.
— Ron Howard (3/1/1954)

March 2
We think we're in the present, but
we aren't. The present we know is
only a movie of the past.
— Tom Wolfe (3/2/1931)

March 3
The women like me because I don't
look like a girl who would steal a
husband—at least not for long.
— Jean Harlow (3/3/1911)

March 4
One loss is good for the soul. Too
many losses are not good for the
coach.   — Knute Rockne (3/4/1888)

March 5
Whatever it is that makes a person
charming, it needs to remain a
mystery. — Rex Harrison (3/5/1908)

March 6
I have known what it was like to be
hungry, but I always went right to a
restaurant.
— Ring Lardner (3/6/1885)

March 7
I'm fifty-five, I'm overweight, I'm
baldheaded, I'm corny—and I'm on
top of the heap.
— Willard Scott (3/7/1934)

March 8
A smart girl is one who knows how
to play tennis, piano, and dumb.
— Lynn Redgrave (3/8/1943)

March 9
A writer is someone who always sells.
An author is one who writes a book
that makes a big splash.
— Mickey Spillane (3/9/1918)

March 10
People have started to call me Miss
Stone instead of just Sharon, which
I'm sure is a combination of my age
and my attitude.
— Sharon Stone (3/10/1958)

March 11
The impossible often has a kind of
integrity which the merely
improbable lacks.
— Douglas Adams (3/11/1952)

March 12
I'm trying to be a public figure and at
the same time be average. It's like
proclaiming my ordinariness.
— James Taylor (3/12/1948)

March 13
Happiness is the overcoming of not unknown obstacles toward a known goal. —L. Ron Hubbard (3/13/1911)

March 14
Only two things are infinite, the universe and human stupidity, and I'm not sure about the former.
—Albert Einstein (3/14/1879)

March 15
If I ever needed a brain transplant, I'd choose a sportswriter because I'd want a brain that had never been used.
—Norm van Brocklin (3/15/1926)

March 16
People hate me because I am a multifaceted, talented, wealthy, internationally famous genius.
—Jerry Lewis (3/16/1926)

March 17
I've given my memoirs far more thought than any of my marriages. You can't divorce a book.
—Gloria Swanson (3/17/1899)

March 18
A healthy male adult bore consumes each year one and a half times his own weight in others' patience.
—John Updike (3/18/1932)

March 19
In America everything goes and nothing matters, while in Europe nothing goes and everything matters.
—Philip Roth (3/19/1933)

March 20
You should never wear your best trousers when you go out to fight for liberty and truth.
—Henrik Ibsen (3/20/1828)

March 21
I'm not the kind of person who'd get a cook and a trainer. If I do, call me up and remind me what I just said.
—Rosie O'Donnell (3/21/1962)

March 22
I prefer neurotic people. I like to hear rumblings beneath the surface.
—Stephen Sondheim (3/22/1930)

March 23
Love is a fire, but whether it is going to warm your hearth or burn down your house, you can never tell.
—Joan Crawford (3/23/1908)

March 24
I'd rather wake up in the middle of nowhere than in any city on Earth.
—Steve McQueen (3/24/1930)

March 25
There's many a bestseller that could have been prevented by a good teacher.
—Flannery O'Connor (3/25/1925)

March 26
By working faithfully eight hours a day, you may eventually get to be boss and work twelve hours a day.
—Robert Frost (3/26/1874)

March 27
I steal from everything. Great artists steal; they don't do homages.
—Quentin Tarantino (3/27/1963)

March 28

When I do an up-tempo song, I have to make it lilt like a woman will twist when she's walking down the street.
—Reba McEntire (3/28/1955)

March 29

With man-made talent, you have to work very hard. With God-given talent, you just touch it up once in a while.
—Pearl Bailey (3/29/1918)

March 30

I'm old. I'm young. I'm intelligent. I'm stupid. My tide goes in and out.
—Warren Beatty (3/30/1937)

March 31

When you have the facts on your side, argue the facts. When you have the law on your side, argue the law. When you have neither, holler.
—Al Gore (3/31/1948)

April 1

My whole career has been devoted to keeping people from knowing me.
—Lon Chaney (4/1/1883)

April 2

I am thirty years old, but I read at the thirty-four-year-old level.
—Dana Carvey (4/2/1955)

April 3

The really frightening thing about middle age is the knowledge that you'll grow out of it.
—Doris Day (4/3/1924)

April 4

If one is lucky, a solitary fantasy can totally transform one million realities.
—Maya Angelou (4/4/1928)

April 5

There were times my pants were so thin I could sit on a dime and tell if it was heads or tails.
—Spencer Tracy (4/5/1900)

April 6

A song is a memory you can listen to, a memory captured in the least amount of words.
—Merle Haggard (4/6/1937)

April 7

Gossip is the art of saying nothing in a way that leaves practically nothing unsaid.
—Walter Winchell (4/7/1897)

April 8

I have a daughter who goes to SMU. She could've gone to UCLA, but it's one more letter she'd have to remember.
—Shecky Greene (4/8/1926)

April 9

I wish that people who have difficulty communicating would just shut up about it.
—Tom Lehrer (4/9/1928)

April 10

A man's home may seem to be his castle on the outside; inside, it is more often his nursery.
—Clare Boothe Luce (4/10/1903)

April 11

The first requirement of a statesman is that he be dull. This is not always easy to achieve.

—Dean Acheson (4/11/1893)

April 12

Success is always temporary. When all is said and done, the only thing you'll have left is your character.

—Vince Gill (4/12/1957)

April 13

The most valuable of all talents is that of never using two words when one will do.

—Thomas Jefferson (4/13/1743)

April 14

I'm no different from anybody else with two arms, two legs, and forty-two hundred hits.

—Pete Rose (4/14/1941)

April 15

"Summer afternoon": to me those have always been the two most beautiful words in the English language.

—Henry James (4/15/1843)

April 16

There are more valid facts and details in works of art than there are in history books.

—Charlie Chaplin (4/16/1889)

April 17

Politicians are the same everywhere. They promise to build bridges even where there are no rivers.

—Nikita Khrushchev (4/17/1894)

April 18

When I was a boy, I was told that anybody could become president; I'm beginning to believe it.

—Clarence Darrow (4/18/1857)

April 19

People down South are incredibly polite. Even their war was civil.

—Dudley Moore (4/19/1935)

April 20

I'm tired of thinking I have to rip my heart out for every character.

—Jessica Lange (4/20/1949)

April 21

They say an Englishman's home is his castle. What I want is to turn my castle into a home.

—Queen Elizabeth II (4/21/1926)

April 22

You lie to two people in your life: your girlfriend and the police. Everyone else you tell the truth.

—Jack Nicholson (4/22/1937)

April 23

I may be a living legend, but that sure don't help when I've got to change a flat tire.

—Roy Orbison (4/23/1936)

April 24

The best way to get husbands to do anything is to suggest that perhaps they're too old to do it.

—Shirley MacLaine (4/24/1934)

April 25

I'm an actor, not a star. Stars are people who live in Hollywood and have heart-shaped swimming pools.

—Al Pacino (4/25/1940)

April 26
Having a baby is like taking your lower lip and forcing it over your head. —Carol Burnett (4/26/1936)

April 27
I know only two tunes. One of them is "Yankee Doodle," and the other isn't. —Ulysses S. Grant (4/27/1822)

April 28
In New York crime is getting worse. I was there the other day. The Statue of Liberty had both hands up.
—Jay Leno (4/28/1950)

April 29
Humans should have fear of flying the same way fish should have fear of driving. —Jerry Seinfeld (4/29/1955)

April 30
I'm a country songwriter and we write cry-in-your-beer songs. That's what we do.
—Willie Nelson (4/30/1933)

May 1
If they try to rush me, I always say, "I've only got one other speed, and it's slower."
—Glenn Ford (5/1/1916)

May 2
There are only two things a child will share willingly—communicable diseases and his mother's age.
—Benjamin Spock (5/2/1903)

May 3
Old age is like a plane flying through a storm. Once you are aboard there is nothing you can do.
—Golda Meir (5/3/1898)

May 4
Football combines the worst features of American life—frantic violence punctuated by committee meetings.
—George Will (5/4/1941)

May 5
I believe that if ever I had to practice cannibalism, I might manage if there were enough tarragon around.
—James Beard (5/5/1903)

May 6
When you're down and out, something always turns up—and it's usually the noses of your friends.
—Orson Welles (5/6/1915)

May 7
I could have played two or three more years. All I needed was a leg transplant.
—Johnny Unitas (5/7/1933)

May 8
It's a recession when your neighbor loses his job; it's a depression when you lose your own.
—Harry S Truman (5/8/1884)

May 9
Know what you love and do what you love. If you don't do what you love, you're just wasting your time.
—Billy Joel (5/9/1949)

May 10
If you're writing songs, there are two things that you just don't write about: politics and religion. We write about both. —Bono (5/10/1960)

May 11
There's an element of truth in every idea that lasts long enough to be called corny.
—Irving Berlin (5/11/1888)

May 12
When driving, anybody going slower than you is an idiot, and anybody going faster than you is a moron.
—George Carlin (5/12/1937)

May 13
People at school told me I couldn't make it, that I would end up making potholders.
—Stevie Wonder (5/13/1950)

May 14
The better the singer's voice, the harder it is to believe what they're saying, so I used my faults to an advantage.
—David Byrne (5/14/1952)

May 15
If you pound on a door hard enough, long enough, often enough, sooner or later somebody will open it.
—Chazz Palminteri (5/15/1951)

May 16
Get as much experience as you can, so that you're ready when luck works. That's the luck.
—Henry Fonda (5/16/1905)

May 17
You do one bad thing a year and it gets talked about for the rest of your life.
—Debra Winger (5/17/1955)

May 18
The things one says are all unsuccessful attempts to say something else.
—Bertrand Russell (5/18/1872)

May 19
The main dangers in this life are the people who want to change everything ... or nothing.
—Nancy Astor (5/19/1879)

May 20
Television is the kind of thing you pay attention to if you wish, and if you don't, you go to clean out your drawers.
—Cher (5/20/1946)

May 21
When you work seven days a week, fourteen hours a day, you get lucky.
—Armand Hammer (5/21/1898)

May 22
Mediocrity knows nothing higher than itself, but talent instantly recognizes genius.
—Arthur Conan Doyle (5/22/1859)

May 23
The problem with beauty is that it's like being born rich and getting poorer.
—Joan Collins (5/23/1933)

May 24
Whenever I hear about another Elvis sighting, it gives me a headache.
—Priscilla Presley (5/24/1946)

May 25
A hero is no braver than an ordinary man, but he is brave five minutes longer.
—Ralph Waldo Emerson (5/25/1803)

May 26
Nobody should come to the movies
unless he believes in heroes.
—John Wayne (5/26/1907)

May 27
The nice thing about being a
celebrity is that if you bore people
they think it's their fault.
—Henry Kissinger (5/27/1923)

May 28
Most marriages don't add two people
together. They subtract one from the
other. —Ian Fleming (5/28/1908)

May 29
Show me a man who plays a good
game of golf, and I'll show you a
man who's neglecting something.
—John F. Kennedy (5/29/1917)

May 30
Women keep a special corner of their
hearts for sins they have never
committed.
—Cornelia Otis Skinner (5/30/1901)

May 31
The trouble with most of us is that
we would rather be ruined by praise
than saved by criticism.
—Norman Vincent Peale (5/31/1898)

June 1
Hollywood's a place where they'll pay
you a thousand dollars for a kiss, and
fifty cents for your soul.
—Marilyn Monroe (6/1/1926)

June 2
There is a good deal too strange to
be believed; nothing is too strange to
have happened.
—Thomas Hardy (6/2/1840)

June 3
If your point of view is right, your
allure will take care of itself.
—Paulette Goddard (6/3/1911)

June 4
Flops are a part of life's menu and
I've never been a girl to miss out on
any of the courses.
—Rosalind Russell (6/4/1911)

June 5
Where else in society do you have
the license to eavesdrop on so many
different conversations as you have in
journalism?
—Bill Moyers (6/5/1934)

June 6
If you are possessed by an idea, you
find it expressed everywhere—you
even smell it.
—Thomas Mann (6/6/1875)

June 7
Find out who you are and what you
stand for, and learn the difference
between right and wrong; be able to
weigh things. —Prince (6/7/1958)

June 8
I hate housework! You make the
beds, you do the dishes—and six
months later you have to start all
over again. —Joan Rivers (6/8/1937)

June 9
I talk to myself because I like dealing
with a better class of people.
—Jackie Mason (6/9/1934)

June 10
When a man opens the car door for his wife, it's either a new car or a new wife.
—Prince Philip (6/10/1921)

June 11
A school without football is in danger of deteriorating into a medieval study hall.
—Vince Lombardi (6/11/1913)

June 12
It's amazing how many people beat you at golf now that you're no longer president.
—George Bush (6/12/1924)

June 13
I've seen women in gyms who must be working out somewhere else to look good enough to come to the gym.   —Tim Allen (6/13/1953)

June 14
People may not always think big themselves, but they can still get very excited by those who do.
—Donald Trump (6/14/1946)

June 15
We campaign in poetry, but when we're elected we're forced to govern in prose.
—Mario Cuomo (6/15/1932)

June 16
True love comes quietly, without banners or flashing lights. If you hear bells, get your ears checked.
—Erich Segal (6/16/1937)

June 17
Harpists spend ninety percent of their lives tuning their harps and ten percent playing out of tune.
—Igor Stravinsky (6/17/1882)

June 18
It's good to go to the movies alone because once you get there, you're not alone. You're at the movies.
—Roger Ebert (6/18/1942)

June 19
Many a man wishes he were strong enough to tear a telephone book in half—especially if he has a teenage daughter.
—Guy Lombardo (6/19/1902)

June 20
The public has always expected me to be a playboy, and a decent chap never lets his public down.
—Errol Flynn (6/20/1909)

June 21
Three o'clock is always too late or too early for anything you want to do.   —Jean-Paul Sartre (6/21/1905)

June 22
France is the only country where the money falls apart and you can't tear the toilet paper.
—Billy Wilder (6/22/1906)

June 23
If you don't like something about yourself, change it. If you can't change it, accept it.
—Ted Shackelford (6/23/1946)

June 24
Speak when you are angry and you will make the best speech you will ever regret.
—Ambrose Bierce (6/24/1842)

June 25
Autobiography is only to be trusted when it reveals something disgraceful.
—George Orwell (6/25/1903)

June 26
The young do not know enough to be prudent, and therefore they attempt the impossible—and achieve it. —Pearl Buck (6/26/1892)

June 27
The activist is not the man who says the river is dirty. The activist is the man who cleans up the river.
—Ross Perot (6/27/1930)

June 28
As long as the world keeps turning and spinning, we're gonna be dizzy and we're gonna make mistakes.
—Mel Brooks (6/28/1926)

June 29
When you're in love it's the most glorious two-and-a-half days of your life. —Richard Lewis (6/29/1947)

June 30
What else am I going to do, be a nuclear scientist? All I know how to do is fight.
—Mike Tyson (6/30/1966)

July 1
You have to have great pain and unhappiness—otherwise, how would you know when you're happy?
—Leslie Caron (7/1/1931)

July 2
Thank God when they went through my closets they found shoes, not skeletons.
—Imelda Marcos (7/2/1931)

July 3
There is a breed of fashion models who weigh no more than an abridged dictionary. —Dave Barry (7/3/1947)

July 4
One of the best ways to measure people is to watch the way they behave when something free is offered. —Ann Landers (7/4/1918)

July 5
The greatest masterpiece in literature is only a dictionary out of order.
—Jean Cocteau (7/5/1889)

July 6
A woman is like a tea bag; you never know how strong she is until she gets in hot water.
—Nancy Reagan (7/6/1921)

July 7
I never threw an illegal pitch. The trouble is, once in a while I toss one that ain't never been seen by this generation.
—Satchel Paige (7/7/1906)

July 8
Good management consists of showing average people how to do the work of superior people.
—John D. Rockefeller (7/8/1839)

July 9
When you get past fifty, you have to decide whether to keep your face or your figure. I kept my face.
—Barbara Cartland (7/9/1901)

July 10
People wish to learn to swim and at the same time to keep one foot on the ground.
—Marcel Proust (7/10/1871)

July 11
I know a lot of people think I'm dumb. Well, at least I ain't no educated fool.
—Leon Spinks (7/11/1953)

July 12
I don't know the key to success, but the key to failure is trying to please everybody. —Bill Cosby (7/12/1937)

July 13
I don't use any method. I'm from the "let's pretend" school of acting.
—Harrison Ford (7/13/1942)

July 14
My basic view of things is not to have any basic view of things.
—Ingmar Bergman (7/14/1918)

July 15
It's all right to hold a conversation, but you should let go of it now and then. —Richard Armour (7/15/1906)

July 16
When two people love each other, they don't look at each other, they look in the same direction.
—Ginger Rogers (7/16/1911)

July 17
When I go to the beauty parlor, I always use the emergency entrance. Sometimes I just go for an estimate.
—Phyllis Diller (7/17/1917)

July 18
If a man's character is to be abused, say what you will, there's nobody like a relation to do the business.
—William Thackeray (7/18/1811)

July 19
Painting is easy when you don't know how, but very difficult when you do. —Edgar Degas (7/19/1834)

July 20
The only time a woman really succeeds in changing a man is when he's a baby.
—Natalie Wood (7/20/1938)

July 21
What is moral is what you feel good after, and what is immoral is what you feel bad after.
—Ernest Hemingway (7/21/1899)

July 22
If the zoo is closed, come over to the Senate. You'll get the same kind of feeling and you won't have to pay.
—Bob Dole (7/22/1923)

July 23
Chess is as elaborate a waste of human intelligence as you can find outside an advertising agency.
—Raymond Chandler (7/23/1888)

July 24
Women must try to do things as men have tried. When they fail, their failure must be but a challenge to others.
—Amelia Earhart (7/24/1898)

July 25
Don't forget about yourself and all of a sudden become what other people see you as—someone's relative.
—Roger Clinton (7/25/1956)

July 26
I'd like to come back as an oyster. Then I'd only have to be good from September until April.
—Gracie Allen (7/26/1906)

July 27
I don't want to achieve immortality by making the Hall of Fame. I want to achieve immortality by not dying.
—Leo Durocher (7/27/1906)

July 28
That's one of the tragedies of this life, that the men who are most in need of a beating up are always enormous.
—Rudy Vallee (7/28/1901)

July 29
Getting kicked out of the American Bar Association is like getting kicked out of the Book-of-the-Month Club.
—Melvin Belli (7/29/1907)

July 30
The secret of managing is to keep the guys who hate you away from the ones who are undecided.
—Casey Stengel (7/30/1890)

July 31
Blessed is he who expects no gratitude, for he shall not be disappointed.
—William Bennett (7/31/1943)

August 1
Truth is something you stumble into when you think you're going someplace else.
—Jerry Garcia (8/1/1942)

August 2
Children have never been very good at listening to their elders, but they have never failed to imitate them.
—James Baldwin (8/2/1924)

August 3
I love the challenge of starting at zero each day and seeing how much I can accomplish.
—Martha Stewart (8/3/1941)

August 4
Poetry lifts the veil from the hidden beauty of the world.
—Percy Bysshe Shelley (8/4/1792)

August 5
Critics have never been able to discover a unifying theme in my films. For that matter, neither have I.
—John Huston (8/5/1906)

August 6
The secret of staying young is to live honestly, eat slowly, and lie about your age.   —Lucille Ball (8/6/1911)

August 7
The highlight of my childhood was making my brother laugh so hard that food came out of his nose.
—Garrison Keillor (8/7/1942)

August 8
I decided to become an actor because I was failing in school and I needed the credits.
—Dustin Hoffman (8/8/1937)

August 9
It was only when I started to shave my head and dress differently that I realized I had a voice as to who I was. —Gillian Anderson (8/9/1968)

August 10
Blessed are the young, for they shall inherit the national debt.
—Herbert Hoover (8/10/1874)

August 11
Being defeated is often a temporary condition. Giving up is what makes it permanent.
—Marilyn vos Savant (8/11/1946)

August 12
The way to make a film is to begin with an earthquake and work up to a climax.
—Cecil B. DeMille (8/12/1881)

August 13
After "The Wizard of Oz" I was typecast as a lion, and there aren't all that many parts for lions.
—Bert Lahr (8/13/1895)

August 14
When you study philosophy in school, you remember just enough to screw you up for the rest of your life.
—Steve Martin (8/14/1945)

August 15
I have trouble with toast. Toast is very difficult. You have to watch it all the time or it burns up.
—Julia Child (8/15/1912)

August 16
I always make the worst-dressed list. It is kind of nice having something you can count on.
—Madonna (8/16/1958)

August 17
When choosing between two evils, I always like to take the one I've never tried before.
—Mae West (8/17/1892)

August 18
In Hollywood, all marriages are happy. It's trying to live together afterward that causes the problems.
—Shelley Winters (8/18/1922)

August 19
Middle age is when you've met so many people that every new person you meet reminds you of someone else. —Ogden Nash (8/19/1902)

August 20
I dare to be great. The man without imagination stands unhurt and has no wings. —Don King (8/20/1931)

August 21

I look for songs that say what every man would like to be able to say, and every woman would like to hear.
—Kenny Rogers (8/21/1938)

August 22

You don't have to burn books to destroy a culture. Just get people to stop reading them.
—Ray Bradbury (8/22/1920)

August 23

The scientific theory I like best is that the rings of Saturn are composed entirely of lost airline luggage. —Mark Russell (8/23/1932)

August 24

I knew I was grown up when I ran back into our burned-out house to put on make-up for the cute firemen.
—Marlee Matlin (8/24/1965)

August 25

Writing about music is like dancing about architecture—it's a really stupid thing to want to do.
—Elvis Costello (8/25/1955)

August 26

A screenwriter is a man who is being tortured to confess and has nothing to confess.
—Christopher Isherwood (8/26/1904)

August 27

I don't want any yes-men around me. I want everybody to tell me the truth even if it costs them their jobs.
—Samuel Goldwyn (8/27/1882)

August 28

One never goes so far as when one doesn't know where one is going.
—Johann Wolfgang von Goethe (8/28/1749)

August 29

I wouldn't have lived my life the way I did if I was going to worry about what people were going to say.
—Ingrid Bergman (8/29/1915)

August 30

All I want out of life is that when I walk down the street, folks will say, "There goes the greatest hitter who ever lived."
—Ted Williams (8/30/1918)

August 31

I'm proud to be paying taxes in the United States. The only thing is, I could be as proud for half the money.
—Arthur Godfrey (8/31/1903)

September 1

I worry that the person who thought up Muzak may be thinking up something else.
—Lily Tomlin (9/1/1939)

September 2

I'm a meathead. I can't help it, man. You've got smart people and you've got dumb people.
—Keanu Reeves (9/2/1964)

September 3

TV cameras seem to add ten pounds to me, so I make it a policy never to eat TV cameras.
—Kitty Carlisle (9/3/1915)

September 4
In times like these, it helps to recall that there have always been times like these. —Paul Harvey (9/4/1918)

September 5
A collision is what happens when two motorists go after the same pedestrian.
—Bob Newhart (9/5/1929)

September 6
Whenever you're sitting across from some important person, always picture him sitting there in a suit of long red underwear.
—Joseph Kennedy (9/6/1888)

September 7
As you get older, you dig deeper into the creative well to find out what the real source is.
—Chrissie Hynde (9/7/1951)

September 8
The trouble with telling a good story is that it invariably reminds the other fellow of a bad one.
—Sid Caesar (9/8/1922)

September 9
Historians are like deaf people who go on answering questions that no one has asked them.
—Leo Tolstoy (9/9/1828)

September 10
I have a tip that can take five strokes off anyone's golf game: it's called an eraser. —Arnold Palmer (9/10/1929)

September 11
Every man I hire is brighter than me. After all, if I'm as smart as you are, I don't need you.
—Bear Bryant (9/11/1913)

September 12
Many a man has fallen in love with a girl in a light so dim he would not have chosen a suit by it.
—Maurice Chevalier (9/12/1888)

September 13
It is far more impressive when others discover your good qualities without your help.
—Judith Martin (9/13/1938)

September 14
I never wanted to be a success, for the very good reason that if I weren't a success, I would be unhappy.
—Sam Neill (9/14/1947)

September 15
An archaeologist is the best husband any woman can have; the older she gets, the more interested he is in her.
—Agatha Christie (9/15/1890)

September 16
At my age, I only remember two things: ladies are pretty and money pays the bills if you can get it.
—B.B. King (9/16/1925)

September 17
I like being a famous writer. Problem is, every once in a while you have to write something.
—Ken Kesey (9/17/1935)

September 18
A cucumber should be well sliced, dressed with pepper and vinegar, and then thrown out.
—Samuel Johnson (9/18/1709)

September 19
If you've got one good wiper blade, you're in good shape—as long as it's on the driver's side.
—Trisha Yearwood (9/19/1964)

September 20
Sex appeal is fifty percent what you've got and fifty percent what people think you've got.
—Sophia Loren (9/20/1934)

September 21
Most of my novels have been plain fiction for plain folks, the literary equivalent of a Big Mac and large fries.
—Stephen King (9/21/1947)

September 22
Talking about your troubles is no good. Eighty percent of your friends don't care and the rest are glad.
—Tommy Lasorda (9/22/1927)

September 23
You write the song just for yourself, but it's no good unless you play it for somebody else.
—Bruce Springsteen (9/23/1949)

September 24
You don't write because you want to say something; you write because you've got something to say.
—F. Scott Fitzgerald (9/24/1896)

September 25
Show me someone who never gossips, and I'll show you someone who isn't interested in people.
—Barbara Walters (9/25/1931)

September 26
I hate exercise. To say you get up at four o'clock in the morning and like to exercise, you'd be psychotic.
—Jack LaLanne (9/26/1914)

September 27
Perfection irritates as well as it attracts, in fiction as in life.
—Louis Auchincloss (9/27/1917)

September 28
Abstract art is a product of the untalented sold by the unprincipled to the utterly bewildered.
—Al Capp (9/28/1909)

September 29
It's the lazy people who invented the wheel and the bicycle because they didn't like walking or carrying things.
—Lech Walesa (9/29/1943)

September 30
I've known all my life I could take a bunch of words and throw them up in the air and they would come down just right.
—Truman Capote (9/30/1924)

October 1
My doctor gave me six months to live, but when I couldn't pay the bill, he gave me six months more.
—Walter Matthau (10/1/1920)

October 2

Age is not a particularly interesting subject. Anyone can get old. All you have to do is live long enough.

—Groucho Marx (10/2/1890)

October 3

Half of the American people never read a newspaper. Half never vote for president. One hopes it is the same half. —Gore Vidal (10/3/1925)

October 4

If you need a ceiling painted, a chariot race run, a city besieged, or the Red Sea parted, you think of me.

—Charlton Heston (10/4/1922)

October 5

It's easy to have principles when you're rich. The important thing is to have principles when you're poor.

—Ray Kroc (10/5/1902)

October 6

Hollywood is where they write the alibis before they write the story.

—Carole Lombard (10/6/1909)

October 7

An expert is a man who has made all the mistakes which can be made in a very narrow field.

—Niels Bohr (10/7/1885)

October 8

I believe that kids as well as adults are entitled to books of no socially redeeming value.

—R.L. Stine (10/8/1943)

October 9

When I was a Beatle, I thought we were the best group in the world, and believing that is what made us what we were.

—John Lennon (10/9/1940)

October 10

The moment of victory is much too short to live for that and nothing else.

—Martina Navratilova (10/10/1956)

October 11

I have spent many years of my life in opposition and I rather like the role.

—Eleanor Roosevelt (10/11/1884)

October 12

Sometimes when I speak I say "we," because I mean me and my voice. We are two different things.

—Luciano Pavarotti (10/12/1935)

October 13

Standing in the middle of the road is very dangerous; you get knocked down by the traffic from both sides.

—Margaret Thatcher (10/13/1925)

October 14

I'm living so far beyond my income that we may almost be said to be living apart.

—e.e. cummings (10/14/1894)

October 15

Has anybody ever seen a drama critic in the daytime? Of course not! They come out after dark, up to no good.

—P.G. Wodehouse (10/15/1881)

October 16

There are many things that we would throw away if we were not afraid that others might pick them up.
—Oscar Wilde (10/16/1854)

October 17

The theater is so endlessly fascinating because it's so accidental. It's so much like life.
—Arthur Miller (10/17/1915)

October 18

Canada is a country whose main exports are hockey players and cold fronts.
—Pierre Trudeau (10/18/1919)

October 19

Having your book turned into a movie is like seeing your oxen turned into bouillon cubes.
—John le Carré (10/19/1931)

October 20

I always wanted to get into politics, but I was never light enough to make the team.
—Art Buchwald (10/20/1925)

October 21

I'm a product of Hollywood. Fantasy is not unnatural to me; it's my reality.
—Carrie Fisher (10/21/1956)

October 22

If you try to measure the future, you will never risk the present.
—Catherine Deneuve (10/22/1943)

October 23

I don't like it when people just call me "Weird." I'm not on a first-adjective basis with anybody.
—"Weird" Al Yankovic (10/23/1959)

October 24

The four most dramatic words in the English language: "Act One, Scene One."
—Moss Hart (10/24/1904)

October 25

Every child is an artist. The problem is how to remain an artist once he grows up.
—Pablo Picasso (10/25/1881)

October 26

I apparently remind some people of their mother-in-law or their boss or something.
—Hillary Clinton (10/26/1947)

October 27

I find it rather easy to portray a businessman. Being bland, rather cruel, and incompetent comes naturally to me.
—John Cleese (10/27/1939)

October 28

To act with my clothes on is a performance; to act with my clothes off is a documentary.
—Julia Roberts (10/28/1967)

October 29

Boys are more susceptible to seduction. They're wimps when it comes to that kind of stuff.
—Winona Ryder (10/29/1971)

October 30

A human being's first responsibility is to shake hands with himself.
—Henry Winkler (10/30/1945)

October 31
A tough lesson in life that one has to learn is that not everybody wishes you well.
—Dan Rather (10/31/1931)

November 1
It's never been an industry secret that show business is exactly like high school, except with money.
—Jenny McCarthy (11/1/1972)

November 2
I can't say I was ever lost, but I was bewildered once for three days.
—Daniel Boone (11/2/1734)

November 3
Someday I'd like a part where I can lean my elbow against a mantelpiece and have a cocktail.
—Charles Bronson (11/3/1922)

November 4
We can't all be heroes because somebody has to sit on the curb and clap as they go by.
—Will Rogers (11/4/1879)

November 5
Times change. Nowadays it's a woman who's faster on the draw, and she can prove it at any bank window.
—Roy Rogers (11/5/1912)

November 6
Nerves provide me with energy. It's when I don't have them, when I feel at ease, that I get worried.
—Mike Nichols (11/6/1931)

November 7
Charm is a way of getting the answer "yes" without asking a clear question.
—Albert Camus (11/7/1913)

November 8
The world can forgive practically anything except people who mind their own business.
—Margaret Mitchell (11/8/1900)

November 9
In the deepest sense, the search for extraterrestrial intelligence is a search for ourselves.
—Carl Sagan (11/9/1934)

November 10
An actor is something less than a man, while an actress is something more than a woman.
—Richard Burton (11/10/1925)

November 11
High school is closer to the core of the American experience than anything else I can think of.
—Kurt Vonnegut (11/11/1922)

November 12
The freedom of the press works in such a way that there is not much freedom from it.
—Grace Kelly (11/12/1929)

November 13
Politics is perhaps the only profession for which no preparation is thought necessary. —Robert Louis Stevenson (11/13/1850)

November 14
I sometimes wonder if two thirds of the globe is covered in red carpet.
—Prince Charles (11/14/1948)

November 15

I hate flowers. I paint them because they're cheaper than models and they don't move.

—Georgia O'Keeffe (11/15/1887)

November 16

The kind of doctor I want is one who, when he's not examining me, is home studying medicine.

—George S. Kaufman (11/16/1889)

November 17

I'm notorious for giving a bad interview. I'm an actor and I can't help but feel I'm boring when I'm on as myself.

—Rock Hudson (11/17/1925)

November 18

The answers you get from literature depend upon the questions you pose.

—Margaret Atwood (11/18/1939)

November 19

There is no politician in India daring enough to explain to the masses that cows can be eaten.

—Indira Gandhi (11/19/1917)

November 20

A professional is someone who can do his best work when he doesn't feel like it.

—Alistair Cooke (11/20/1908)

November 21

Comedy breaks down walls. It opens up people. If you're good, you can fill up those openings with something positive.

—Goldie Hawn (11/21/1945)

November 22

Since a politician never believes what he says, he is always astonished when others do.

—Charles de Gaulle (11/22/1890)

November 23

When I was nine, I played the Demon King in "Cinderella," and it launched me on a long and happy life of being a monster.

—Boris Karloff (11/23/1887)

November 24

Ask yourself: What is the worst that can happen? Then prepare to accept it. Then proceed to improve on the worst. —Dale Carnegie (11/24/1888)

November 25

As I grow older, I pay less attention to what men say. I just watch what they do.

—Andrew Carnegie (11/25/1835)

November 26

You must love and care for yourself, because that's when the best comes out.   —Tina Turner (11/26/1939)

November 27

The English instinctively admire any man who has no talent and is modest about it. —James Agee (11/27/1909)

November 28

My work is visionary or imaginative. That which can be explained to the idiot is not worth my care.

—William Blake (11/28/1757)

November 29
They should put expiration dates on clothes so we would know when they go out of style.
—Garry Shandling (11/29/1949)

November 30
Part of the secret of success in life is to eat what you like and let the food fight it out inside.
—Mark Twain (11/30/1835)

December 1
I cheated on the final of my metaphysics examination. I looked into the soul of the boy sitting next to me. —Woody Allen (12/1/1935)

December 2
People say to me, "You don't look like an athlete, you look like a person." —Monica Seles (12/2/1973)

December 3
Being a woman is a terribly difficult trade, since it consists principally of dealing with men.
—Joseph Conrad (12/3/1857)

December 4
It is the function of vice to keep virtue within reasonable bounds.
—Samuel Butler (12/4/1835)

December 5
As far as I'm concerned, "whom" is a word that was invented to make everyone sound like a butler.
—Calvin Trillin (12/5/1935)

December 6
I'm a peripheral visionary. I can see into the future but way off to the side. —Steven Wright (12/6/1955)

December 7
Achievement is for senators and scholars. At one time I had ambitions, but I had them removed by a doctor in Buffalo.
—Tom Waits (12/7/1949)

December 8
No man who has wrestled with a self-adjusting card table can ever be quite the man he once was.
—James Thurber (12/8/1894)

December 9
If you want to know about a man, you can find out an awful lot by looking at who he married.
—Kirk Douglas (12/9/1916)

December 10
If I feel physically as if the top of my head were taken off, I know that is poetry.
—Emily Dickinson (12/10/1830)

December 11
The salvation of mankind lies only in making everything the concern of all.
—Alexander Solzhenitsyn (12/11/1918)

December 12
Nothing is more humiliating than to see idiots succeed in enterprises we have failed in.
—Gustave Flaubert (12/12/1821)

December 13
Women will never be as successful as men because they have no wives to advise them.
—Dick Van Dyke (12/13/1925)

December 14
Love is blind. I guess that's why it proceeds by the sense of touch.
—Morey Amsterdam (12/14/1914)

December 15
If you get up early, work late, and pay your taxes, you will get ahead—if you strike oil.
—Jean Paul Getty (12/15/1892)

December 16
Wit is like caviar. It should be served in small, elegant portions and not splashed about like marmalade.
—Noel Coward (12/16/1899)

December 17
Is sloppiness in speech caused by ignorance or apathy? I don't know and I don't care.
—William Safire (12/17/1929)

December 18
Stories don't have a middle or an end anymore. They usually have a beginning that never stops beginning.
—Steven Spielberg (12/18/1947)

December 19
Challenges make you discover things about yourself that you never really knew. —Cicely Tyson (12/19/1933)

December 20
I have a simple principle for the conduct of life—never to resist an adequate temptation.
—Max Lerner (12/20/1902)

December 21
You can run an office without a boss, but you can't run an office without secretaries.
—Jane Fonda (12/21/1937)

December 22
The way you overcome shyness is to become so wrapped up in something that you forget to be afraid.
—Lady Bird Johnson (12/22/1912)

December 23
Running is step by step. If you go step by step, you'll always improve. I like that about running.
—Bill Rodgers (12/23/1947)

December 24
The true meaning of religion is not simply morality but morality touched by emotion.
—Matthew Arnold (12/24/1822)

December 25
If an actor has a message, he should call Western Union. An actor's job is to act, nothing more.
—Humphrey Bogart (12/25/1899)

December 26
If you want to read about love and marriage, you've got to buy two separate books.
—Alan King (12/26/1927)

December 27
The relationship between the make-up man and the film actor is that of accomplices in crime.
—Marlene Dietrich (12/27/1901)

December 28

I would never read a book if it were possible for me to talk half an hour with the man who wrote it.

—Woodrow Wilson (12/28/1856)

December 29

You can't be brave if you've only had wonderful things happen to you.

—Mary Tyler Moore (12/29/1937)

December 30

Borrow trouble for yourself, if that's your nature, but don't lend it to your neighbors.

—Rudyard Kipling (12/30/1865)

December 31

There is nothing more difficult for a truly creative painter than to paint a rose.   —Henri Matisse (12/31/1869)

INDEX

Coward, Noel: 12/16
Crawford, Joan: 3/23
cummings, e.e.: 10/14
Cuomo, Mario: 6/15

Darrow, Clarence: 4/18
Day, Doris: 4/3
Degas, Edgar: 7/19
de Gaulle, Charles: 11/22
DeMille, Cecil B.: 8/12
Deneuve, Catherine: 10/22
Dickens, Charles: 2/7
Dickinson, Emily: 12/10
Dietrich, Marlene: 12/27
Diller, Phyllis: 7/17
Dole, Bob: 7/22
Douglas, Kirk: 12/9
Doyle, Arthur Conan: 5/22
Durocher, Leo: 7/27

Earhart, Amelia: 7/24
Ebert, Roger: 6/18
Einstein, Albert: 3/14
Elizabeth II, Queen: 4/21
Emerson, Ralph Waldo: 5/25

Fields, W.C.: 1/29
Fisher, Carrie: 10/21
Fitzgerald, F. Scott: 9/24
Flaubert, Gustave: 12/12
Fleming, Ian: 5/28
Flynn, Errol: 6/20
Fonda, Henry: 5/16
Fonda, Jane: 12/21
Ford, Glenn: 5/1
Ford, Harrison: 7/13
Foreman, George: 1/10
Franklin, Benjamin: 1/17
Frost, Robert: 3/26

Gable, Clark: 2/1
Gandhi, Indira: 11/19
Garcia, Jerry: 8/1
Getty, Jean Paul: 12/15
Gill, Vince: 4/12

Goddard, Paulette: 6/3
Godfrey, Arthur: 8/31
Goethe, Johann Wolfgang von: 8/28
Goldwater, Barry: 1/1
Goldwyn, Samuel: 8/27
Gore, Al: 3/31
Grant, Cary: 1/18
Grant, Ulysses S.: 4/27
Greene, Shecky: 4/8

Haggard, Merle: 4/6
Hammer, Armand: 5/21
Hardy, Thomas: 6/2
Harlow, Jean: 3/3
Harrison, Rex: 3/5
Hart, Moss: 10/24
Harvey, Paul: 9/4
Hawn, Goldie: 11/21
Hemingway, Ernest: 7/21
Heston, Charlton: 10/4
Hoffman, Dustin: 8/8
Hoover, Herbert: 8/10
Howard, Ron: 3/1
Hubbard, L. Ron: 3/13
Hudson, Rock: 11/17
Huston, John: 8/5
Hynde, Chrissie: 9/7

Ibsen, Henrik: 3/20
Isherwood, Christopher: 8/26

James, Henry: 4/15
James, William: 1/11
Jefferson, Thomas: 4/13
Jobs, Steve: 2/24
Joel, Billy: 5/9
Johnson, Lady Bird: 12/22
Johnson, Samuel: 9/18
Jordan, Michael: 2/17

Karloff, Boris: 11/23
Kaufman, George S.: 11/16
Keillor, Garrison: 8/7
Kelly, Grace: 11/12

Kennedy, John F.: 5/29
Kennedy, Joseph: 9/6
Kesey, Ken: 9/17
Khrushchev, Nikita: 4/17
King, Alan: 12/26
King, B.B.: 9/16
King, Don: 8/20
King, Stephen: 9/21
Kipling, Rudyard: 12/30
Kissinger, Henry: 5/27
Kroc, Ray: 10/5

Lahr, Bert: 8/13
LaLanne, Jack: 9/26
Landers, Ann: 7/4
Lange, Jessica: 4/20
Lardner, Ring: 3/6
Lasorda, Tommy: 9/22
Le Carré, John: 10/19
Lehrer, Tom: 4/9
Lemmon, Jack: 2/8
Lennon, John: 10/9
Leno, Jay: 4/28
Lerner, Max: 12/20
Lewis, Jerry: 3/16
Lewis, Richard: 6/29
Lincoln, Abraham: 2/12
Loggins, Kenny: 1/7
Lombard, Carole: 10/6
Lombardi, Vince: 6/11
Lombardo, Guy: 6/19
Loren, Sophia: 9/20
Louis-Dreyfus, Julia: 1/13
Luce, Clare Boothe: 4/10

MacLaine, Shirley: 4/24
Madonna: 8/16
Mann, Thomas: 6/6
Marcos, Imelda: 7/2
Martin, Judith: 9/13
Martin, Steve: 8/14
Marvin, Lee: 2/19
Marx, Groucho: 10/2
Mason, Jackie: 6/9
Matisse, Henri: 12/31

Matlin, Marlee: 8/24
Matthau, Walter: 10/1
Maugham, W. Somerset: 1/25
McCarthy, Jenny: 11/1
McEntire, Reba: 3/28
McQueen, Steve: 3/24
Meir, Golda: 5/3
Merman, Ethel: 1/16
Miller, Arthur: 10/17
Mitchell, Margaret: 11/8
Mondale, Walter: 1/5
Monroe, Marilyn: 6/1
Moore, Dudley: 4/19
Moore, Mary Tyler: 12/29
Moreau, Jeanne: 1/23
Morrison, Toni: 2/18
Moyers, Bill: 6/5

Nash, Ogden: 8/19
Navratilova, Martina: 10/10
Neill, Sam: 9/14
Nelson, Willie: 4/30
Newhart, Bob: 9/5
Newman, Paul: 1/26
Newton, Isaac: 1/4
Nichols, Mike: 11/6
Nicholson, Jack: 4/22
Nicklaus, Jack: 1/21
Nixon, Richard M.: 1/9

O'Connor, Flannery: 3/25
O'Donnell, Rosie: 3/21
O'Keeffe, Georgia: 11/15
Onassis, Aristotle: 1/15
Orbison, Roy: 4/23
Orwell, George: 6/25
Osgood, Charles: 1/8

Pacino, Al: 4/25
Paige, Satchel: 7/7
Palmer, Arnold: 9/10
Palminteri, Chazz: 5/15
Pavarotti, Luciano: 10/12
Peale, Norman Vincent: 5/31
Pepys, Samuel: 2/23

Vallee, Rudy: 7/28
van Brocklin, Norm: 3/15
Van Dyke, Dick: 12/13
Vidal, Gore: 10/3
Vonnegut, Kurt: 11/11
vos Savant, Marilyn: 8/11

Waits, Tom: 12/7
Walesa, Lech: 9/29
Walker, Alice: 2/9
Walters, Barbara: 9/25
Wayne, John: 5/26
Welles, Orson: 5/6
West, Mae: 8/17
Wharton, Edith: 1/24
Wilde, Oscar: 10/16
Wilder, Billy: 6/22

Will, George: 5/4
Williams, Ted: 8/30
Wilson, Woodrow: 12/28
Winchell, Walter: 4/7
Winger, Debra: 5/17
Winkler, Henry: 10/30
Winters, Shelley: 8/18
Wodehouse, P.G.: 10/15
Wolfe, Tom: 3/2
Wonder, Stevie: 5/13
Wood, Natalie: 7/20
Wright, Steven: 12/6

Yankovic, "Weird" Al: 10/23
Yearwood, Trisha: 9/19
Youngman, Henny: 1/12

ABOUT THE AUTHOR

Trip Payne is a freelance puzzlemaker living in Atlanta. Primarily a crossword puzzle constructor, Payne regularly has his creations printed in publications ranging from *The New York Times* to *TV Guide*.

In addition to *365 Mind-Challenging Cryptograms*, Payne is also the author of *Crosswords for Kids* and *Mighty Mini Crosswords*, as well as the coauthor of *The Little Giant Encyclopedia of Word Puzzles*, all published by Sterling.

While he likes many of the quotations in this book, his current favorite celebrity quote is this one from McDonald's founder Ray Kroc: "It requires a certain kind of mind to see beauty in a hamburger bun."

Dan Wenke at Bern-Art Studios

WHAT IS AMERICAN MENSA?

American Mensa
The High IQ Society
One out of 50 people qualifies
for American Mensa ...
Are YOU the One?

American Mensa, Ltd. is an organization for individuals who
have one common trait: a score in the top two percent of the
population on a standardized intelligence test. Over five million
Americans are eligible for membership ... you may be one of
them.

• Looking for intellectual stimulation?
You'll find a good "mental workout" in the *Mensa Bulletin,* our
national magazine. Voice your opinion in the newsletter
published by your local group. And attend activities and gatherings with fascinating programs and engaging conversation.

• Looking for social interaction?
There's something happening on the Mensa calendar almost
daily. These range from lectures to game nights to parties.
Each year, there are over 40 regional gatherings and the
Annual Gathering, where you can meet people, exchange
ideas, and make interesting new friends.

• Looking for others who share your special interest?
Whether your interest might be in computer gaming, Monty

Python, or scuba, there's probably a Mensa Special Interest Group (SIG) for you. There are over 150 SIGs, which are started and maintained by members.

So contact us today to receive a free brochure and application.

American Mensa, Ltd.
1229 Corporate Drive West
Arlington, TX 76006
(800) 66-MENSA
AmericanMensa@mensa.org
www.us.mensa.org

For Canadians, contact:

Mensa Canada Society
329 March Road
Suite 232, Box 11
Kanata, Ontario Canada
K2K 2E1
(613) 599-5897
info@canada.mensa.org

If you don't live in the U.S. and would like to get in touch with your national Mensa, contact:

Mensa International
15 The Ivories
6–8 Northampton Street, Islington
London N1 2HY England